Praise for *Wild Life!*

"Embracing the wild means stepping back and connecting with the larger complexity. By focusing on nature's lesser-known but critical species and the people who work to protect them, *Wild Life!* reminds us of the interconnectedness of all wild beings, and of the role we all play within that complexity."

—ADRIAN GRENIER, UN Environment Goodwill Ambassador, impact investor, and cofounder of Lonely Whale

"An intersectional approach to the protection of both people + planet that seeks to uplift all people and empower Indigenous voices is crucial to restoring the wild! It takes all of us to save the planet—read this book and gain insights from the best!"

—LEAH THOMAS, founder of Intersectional Environmentalist

"We all have our own story to tell, and this book contains stories of species and the incredible people protecting them. It celebrates their quirks and talents, and their importance to the amazing, interconnected system of the wild."

—KARRUECHE TRAN, actor and model

"*Wild Life!* takes us on a fact-based ride through the wild and wonderful world of species that are little known, seldom seen, and in need of more love. Geek out over these animals—they'll definitely grab your attention and take you to places you didn't know existed."

—CARL SAFINA, author of *Becoming Wild: How Animal Cultures Raise Families, Create Beauty, and Achieve Peace*

wild life!

re:wild

with SYD ROBINSON

A Look at Nature's Odd Ducks, Underfrogs, and Other At-Risk Species

ADAMS MEDIA

NEW YORK   LONDON   TORONTO   SYDNEY   NEW DELHI

Adams Media
An Imprint of Simon & Schuster, Inc.
100 Technology Center Drive
Stoughton, Massachusetts 02072

First Adams Media hardcover edition October 2021

ADAMS MEDIA and colophon are trademarks of Simon & Schuster.

For information about special discounts for bulk purchases, please contact Simon & Schuster Special Sales at 1-866-506-1949 or business@simonandschuster.com.

The Simon & Schuster Speakers Bureau can bring authors to your live event. For more information or to book an event contact the Simon & Schuster Speakers Bureau at 1-866-248-3049 or visit our website at www.simonspeakers.com.

Interior design by Sylvia McArdle
Interior photograph credits listed alongside images
Cover photo © Robin Moore

Manufactured in China

10 9 8 7 6 5 4 3 2 1

Library of Congress Cataloging-in-Publication Data
Names: Robinson, Syd, author.
Title: Wild life! / Re:wild with Syd Robinson.
Description: First Adams Media hardcover edition. | Stoughton, MA: Adams Media, 2021.
Identifiers: LCCN 2021013717 | ISBN 9781507216439 (hc) | ISBN 9781507216446 (ebook)
Subjects: LCSH: Endangered species. | Wildlife conservation.
Classification: LCC QL82 .R627 2021 | DDC 591.68--dc23
LC record available at https://lccn.loc.gov/2021013717

ISBN 978-1-5072-1643-9
ISBN 978-1-5072-1644-6 (ebook)

The photos in this book are of animals in their wild homes, where possible, or of animals in a conservation breeding program or accredited zoo, as indicated in the captions. None of the animals in these photos were baited or harmed in any way for the purpose of taking the photo.

The status and population trend information included in this book come from the International Union for Conservation of Nature's Red List of Threatened Species™.

Materials used in the manufacture of this book are certified by the Forest Stewardship Council to reduce environmental impact.

A portion of the proceeds from the sale of this book will aid Re:wild in their mission to protect and restore the wild.

Dedicated to NEMONTE NENQUIMO,
whose bold spirit inspires us to listen to the
Indigenous peoples who are guardians of our
planet, and to cherish and protect our profound
connection with the wild and
all of life on Earth.

We would like to thank the following individuals for offering their expertise and reviewing the profiles pertinent to their work:

Abdullahi H. Ali
Agustín Schiariti
Albert Bertolero
Alexei V. Abramov
Amirrudin B. Ahmad
Amy Deane
Amy Moran
Andrea Piñones
Andrew Smith
Andrew Tilker
Andy Gluesenkamp
Anya Ratnayaka
Arif Setiawan
Axel Hochkirch
Badru Mugerwa
Barb Taylor
Barney Long
Benoit Dodelin
Bradley Watson
Brodie Chiswick
Bronwyn Jeynes
Carlos Henrique Salvador
Carlos Nores
Cecil Jennings
Chien C. Lee
Chris Bowden
Chris Jordan

Clay Bolt
Clive Evans
Cynthia Smith
David Jeggo
David Priddel
David Sischo
Day B Ligon
Deborah Pardo
Denise Risch
Denise Thompson
Douglas Krause
Douglas M. Richardson
Edward Louis
Eli Wyman
Emmanuel Schütz
Esteban Brenes-Mora
Eva Pisano
Hugo Alejandro Herrera Gomez
Ian Hogg
Indraneil Das
Inger Perkins
Jacob Marlin
Jacqueline D. Litzgus
Jake Osborne
James Burton
Jan Schipper

Jenny Daltry
Jessica Lee
James M. Dietz
Jim Sanderson
John Sparks
John Zichy-Woinarski
Jon Paul Rodríguez
Jordi Salmona
Jörg Freyhof
José Tavares
Joseph Eastman
Joshua M. Guilbert
Juan Herrero
Julian Kerbis Peterhans
Julie Harvey
Karen Strier
Keri Parker
Kristina Martz
Laura Ghigliotti
Lauren Augustine
Leandro Castello
Li Ling Ho
Lina Valencia
Liz Brown
Liza Fowler
Lorenzo Rojas-Bracho
Marianne Hartmann-Furter

Marina Rutovskaya
Maurice La Haye
Mic Mayhew
Michael McFadden
Michelle LaRue
Milton Yacelga
Minh Le
Natalia Rossi
Nerida G. Wilson
Nerissa Chao
Nicholas M. Teets
Paul A. Cziko
Peter Paul van Dijk
Petra Kovač-Konrad
PJ Stephenson
Rachel Ashegbofe Ikemeh
Rhys Buckingham
Richard Griffiths
Richard Lewis
Richard Thorns
Rob Holm

Roberto Guidetti
Robin D. Moore
Rogan Colbourne
Roger Key
Roger Safford
Roopali Raghavan
Rosalind Kennerley
S. Blair Hedges
Samuel Turvey
Sandro Lovari
Sarah Lamar
Scott Johnson
Scott Tremor
Sectionov Inov
Serene Chng
Sonja Luz
Stephen P. Kirkman
Sula Vanderplank
Susan M. Cheyne
Teresa Camacho Badani
Thành Nguyễn Văn

Thomas M. Butynski
Thomas Rainwater
Tim Davenport
Tim Faulkner
Tom Espinoza
Treya Picking
Vicky Wilkins
Wes Sechrest

We would also like to thank the following Re:wild editors: Carrie Hutchison, Barney Long, Robin Moore, Devin Murphy, Lindsay Renick Mayer, Kyrsten Stringer, and Wes Sechrest. Thank you also to Macson McGuigan for his critical role in pulling the photos for this book together.

Contents

Africa

North America

South and Central America

Oceana

Antarctica 219

Introduction

From the tiniest mouse to the most colossal whale—and all the whimsical and fantastical animals in between—all living things on our planet are part of Earth's biodiversity. The diversity of life is key to healthy ecosystems, and healthy ecosystems are the immune system of our planet. They curb climate change, prevent catastrophic fires and pandemics, regulate our weather, and ensure a healthy planet for all life on Earth—including humans. Though the extinction of a single species may not spell catastrophe for our planet, each species that vanishes pushes us closer to finding ourselves on an unlivable Earth.

Here's the kicker, though: Ecosystems contain more than plants and animals. YOU play a role too. Everyone you know plays their own critical part in keeping the world keepin' on, and if that sounds really meta...that's because it is. Now is the time to rewild our planet.

What does "rewild" mean? Well, for example, you can rewild your backyard by planting some native trees or plants. You could also rewild mainland Australia by reintroducing the Tasmanian Devil to its ecosystems after being absent for three thousand years. Rewilding is all about restoring and rebalancing the Earth. It's also about rewilding ourselves and reveling in the wonders of the wild. Simply put, that's Re:wild's mission, and that's what we're trying to do with this very cool and very fun book you're currently holding.

In *Wild Life!* we'll introduce you to one hundred animals who fly a little more under the radar. You've probably seen a million books about charismatic megafauna like pandas, lions, and elephants, but what about the little guys whose stories are rarely told, the hidden gems of the natural kingdom? Ever heard of the Pink-Headed Duck? Now you have.

Wild Life! shines a light on the animals you've never heard of, including a few that have been lost to science for decades (we call these "Lost Species"), and encourages you to reimagine our collective role in self-sustaining ecosystems.

In this book, you'll get to know these *underfrogs*—as we like to call them!—from all seven continents, as well as certain "celebrity animals," and even some stories about the people who work on protecting these species every day, aka Re:wild's "guardians." Most of these profiles include beautiful, full-color photographs, but for our "Lost Species" features, we had to get creative by illustrating these animals the best we could.

At Re:wild, we're actively working every single day to protect and restore many of the animals— and their homes—that you'll find in these pages. We do it for our underfrogs, for ourselves, and, most importantly, for all life on Earth—now, and for years to come. We hope that you might want to help too.

Without further ado, we invite you to rewild yourself—and help us rewild the world!

Europe

EUROPEAN HAMSTER

Animal: European Hamster, aka Common Hamster
Class: Mammalia (Mammal)
Species: *Cricetus cricetus*
Status: Critically Endangered
Population Trend: Decreasing

Yup, you guessed it—these little beans are the wild relatives of the pet hamster you might have had growing up! They look like your typical hamster but mixed with a red panda because of their blotchy reddish-blackish coat. While the European Hamster is just as cute and chonky as its domesticated cousin, it is *definitely* not as snuggly. They are quite ferocious, even though they weigh only 1 pound (0.453 kilograms). But wow, are they cute!

From "Common" to Not So Much

The European Hamster, also called the Common Hamster, is actually not all that "common" anymore. Sadly, it recently went from Least Concern to Critically Endangered. While the European Hamster used to be found in cereal fields on löss (loess)/loamy soils and in natural steppes, the intensification of agriculture, climate change, and possibly light pollution have all strained European Hamster populations.

Warmer winters due to climate change are one of the biggest threats to these little expert burrowers. During the typically colder months,

they use their teeny, tiny paws to dig holes that are more than 6 feet (2 meters) deep—quite impressive if you ask us!—and curl up to hibernate there, usually protected by a layer of snow that keeps their winter home nice and insulated. But with these new warmer winters, there's been less snowfall, less protection, and, subsequently, fewer European Hamsters.

Saving a Keystone Species

European Hamsters are what's known as a "keystone species," which means they play a huge role in keeping their ecosystem healthy. If European Hamsters were to disappear, all the animals who eat them would go hungry, and so on and so forth until their whole ecosystem collapses.

There is a glimmer of hope: The European Hamster has been reintroduced in France, Belgium, the Netherlands, and Germany in recent years, and their second comings have seemed to be pretty effective at upping their population! In 2009, the Bern Convention created an action plan to update protection policies for the hamster in those countries. The population is

European Hamster, in a cemetery in Vienna, Austria. Photo © Fabian Fopp

monitored regularly in Western Europe, and has spread to Poland, Czech Republic, Ukraine, and more.

Hopefully, full protection plans will also spread throughout the European Hamster's range, and someday soon the Common Hamster will actually be considered "common" once again.

underfrog ● fact ●

The female hamster's pregnancy only lasts an average of eighteen days!

EUROPEAN BISON

Animal: European Bison, aka Wisent
Class: Mammalia (Mammal)
Species: *Bison bonasus*
Status: Vulnerable
Population Trend: Increasing

The biggest land mammal in all of Europe, the European Bison can tip the scale at anywhere from 705 to 2,200 pounds (between 320 and 1,000 kilograms). The European Bison has a slightly lankier build than the North American Bison, its hair is definitely not as shaggy, and its horns are more curved and cow-like. Basically, it's more suave and, well, *European-looking*.

While European Bison generally prefer open spaces to chomp some grass and freely headbutt one another, they've essentially been forced into little remote forests in Europe over the years.

A Cave Painter's Muse

According to DNA evidence, it's assumed that this big old beefy hunk first appeared over 120,000 years ago. This Wisent (a fancy name for bison) has even been depicted in cave drawings.

You might be wondering: If these big beasts have been around for literally hundreds of thousands of years, how on Earth did they become listed as Vulnerable? Well, we'll tell you: poaching.

While poaching hit the bison the hardest, other causes include the displacement of herds as the result of human settlement and agriculture. These poor guys really can't catch a break.

Super Poopers

The European Bison is a "keystone species." They can eat up to 132 pounds (60 kilograms) of vegetation every day, which keeps landscapes open. They roll around in sandpits and then poop in them. And poop is good! Poop is fertilizer, and fertilizer keeps plants growing. To put it frankly, healthy ecosystems need the European Bison and their poop!

The Białowieża Forest Getaway

Although the European Bison went Extinct in the wild in 1927, experts have been using strategic breeding programs to keep track of them since 1932. And thanks to those last fifty-five bison that were kept in zoos and on private estates, the keystone species miraculously survived!

In 1952 the first bison were released into the Białowieża Forest, a cute little spot on the border of Poland and Belarus. Today, the Białowieża Forest is home to around 1,350 European Bison, with another 4,800 living wild in other parts of Europe, and 2,200 still part of a conservation breeding program for future reintroductions. Progress!

underfrog ●
fact ●

In the early sixteenth century, a Polish king made poaching these bison punishable by the *death penalty*, and only local royalty and their special guests were permitted to hunt them!

European Bison, Shahdag National Park, Azerbaijan.
Photo © Rustam Maharramov, WWF Azerbaijan

RUSSIAN DESMAN

Animal: Russian Desman
Class: Mammalia (Mammal)
Species: *Desmana moschata*
Status: Endangered
Population Trend: Decreasing

The Russian Desman is more or less what you'd get if you imagined crossing a platypus with a mole, and then gave it eyes that looked perpetually shocked. This semiaquatic native to Kazakhstan, Russia, and maybe even Ukraine, spends its days messing around in whatever floodplains it can find its way into! As of right now, only about eight thousand to ten thousand desmans are still wildin' out in these areas, classifying them as Endangered.

Dreading Droughts

Since around the early twentieth century, these bizarre little furballs have been steadily decreasing because of land reclamation, construction, and poaching. Not to mention A LOT of droughts, which have *really* ruined the desman's day. This desman lives in an ambient temperature that drastically changes from season to season, so they're pretty good at adapting, but still—an increase in droughts and lack of floods? No thank you! The Russian Desman has no interest in living—or reproducing, for that matter—in dry, warm places where the water is drying up and shallow!

Saving the Desman

As for conservation efforts, the only thing really helping these guys out is their Status 2 listing in the *Red Data Book of the Russia Federation*, which indicates their population is going down. This status makes hunting them illegal and designates some protected spots just for them! In the middle of the last century, a giant-scale reacclimatization—returning the animals to a habitat where they once lived but then disappeared from—for the desman was carried out. The desman was also released into new but similar habitats to acclimate there.

In the 1990s, Russian politics shifted direction and environmental issues were sadly shoved to the side. Poaching picked up again, and desmans suffered as a consequence. Today, poaching has mostly been shut down. The main issue the Russian Desman faces now is rising temperatures as a result of climate change.

Russian Desman, the Bryansk Forest Nature Reserve, Russia. Photo © Igor Shpileno, Nature Picture Library

Looking ahead, monitoring desman populations is critical, as is preserving their reserves and creating more nurseries to breed desmans in human care. The end goal will be to release the little guys into nature again. The very first Russian Desman nursery is being constructed right now thanks to a presidential grant.

underfrog ●
fact ●

The desman is a riparian species, meaning it depends on rivers and lives in burrows in their banks.

EUROPEAN POND TURTLE

Animal: European Pond Turtle
Class: Reptilia (Reptile)
Species: *Emys orbicularis*
Status: Near Threatened
Population Trend: Unspecified

The European Pond Turtle spends its days just hanging at the pond, lounging on rocks, and basking in the warm glow of the western Palearctic sun. It helps itself to a buffet-style assortment of insects, frogs, and fishes when it's in the mood for a snack, and then goes and basks on another rock.

A Pet Threat

Not everything has been all sunshine and rainbows for this little turtle, though—it faces a plethora of threats, including hunting, and because of the gorgeous yellow flecks on its body, the European Pond Turtle has become an unfortunate target of the European pet trade.

Protecting Their Ponds

The European Pond Turtle is legally protected, and conservation efforts have popped up all over Europe. In Hungary in 2002, the World Wildlife Fund (WWF) launched a turtle protection program that conducted regular habitat surveys and went into schools to raise awareness of the Near Threatened turtle. Germany has also gotten in on the action by focusing on long-term conservation in Brandenburg, and a reintroduction program has been started in Frankfurt.

So far, the most successful attempt to save the European Pond Turtle has been France's reintroduction program. Between 2000 and 2002, France managed to release thirty-five adult European Pond Turtles into Lake Bourget, Savoie. The majority of these turtles survived and went on to make some quaint and incredibly homey nests.

Significant Nutrient Recyclers

Back in the day, turtle populations thrived in droves, and they were architects in their environments. Because there were so many of them, European Pond Turtles played a huge role in reworking soils and pond floors, and dispersing seeds and other nutrients all over their habitats. The gradual decline of the European Pond Turtle means they haven't been able to play their ecological roles to the same extent. In turn, the ponds, lakes, and streams they live in are—*sigh*—not nearly as biodiverse as they once were.

underfrog ●
fact ●

European Pond Turtles found in northern Europe tend to be larger than those found down south.

European Pond Turtle, Danube Delta, Romania. Photo © Magnus Lundgren, Wild Wonders of Europe, Nature Picture Library

OLM

Animal: Olm, aka Cave Salamander
Class: Amphibia (Amphibian)
Species: *Proteus anguinus*
Status: Vulnerable
Population Trend: Decreasing

Olms, or Cave Salamanders, are just about the strangest, most unbelievable animals you could possibly imagine—so strange that locals in Bosnia once believed they were baby dragons! These supposed baby dragons have been around for an estimated 8.8–20 million years and can live longer than a century, but according to scientists, Olms haven't done much at all in that time. One Olm was recorded staying completely still for 2,569 days straight—that's SEVEN YEARS (and two weeks, if we're being really specific!). Olms live in northern Italy, Slovenia, Croatia, Bosnia and Herzegovina, and possibly Montenegro.

Very, VERY Slow and Steady

Being slow and mostly stationary, the Olm, on average, moves about 16 feet (5 meters) per year. Since they've adapted to living in the otherworldly submerged caves of Dinaric karst, Olms have a specific cave-centric skill set. Olms are basically blind but have developed a wild sense of smell, taste, and hearing. Olms also barely need oxygen and can go several years without eating, so there really is no need for them to exert energy. They might have to expend a little energy when it's time to reproduce, but even one gestation period lasts twelve and a half years—so really, there's no rush.

Living Their Karst Life

As far as threats go, karst pollution caused by rain and runoff from waste disposal sites is a big problem for the Olm. The now-Vulnerable Olms rely on having clean water around them and land above them, and since they've gotten so used to karst living over the last several million years, any change in their environment is a total shock to their system.

The Olm was first protected in Slovenia in 1922. Sadly, these restrictions didn't stop people from getting their hands on them, and eventually, the poor Olm found itself in the middle of a nasty black market trade. In 1982, it was put on an endangered species list and protected by the Bern Convention on wildlife protection.

Avoiding Olm-ost Extinct

Nowadays, the Olm is mostly found in caves of Dinaric karst. There are some efforts to breed them in human care, and some other conservationists are testing the environmental DNA in the karst streams to learn more about this ever-whimsical cave salamander—noninvasively, we might add!

underfrog ● fact ●

The Olm has been named one of Slovenia's national treasures and is featured on one of their coins.

Olm, Divje Jezero, Slovenia. Photo © Arne Hodalič, Wild Wonders of Europe, Nature Picture Library

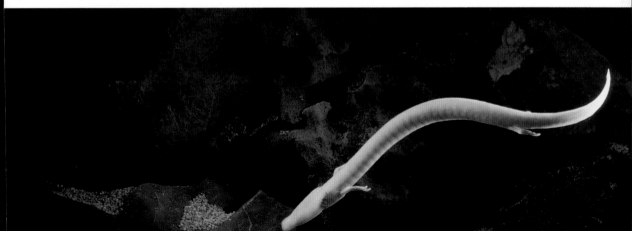

MALLORCAN MIDWIFE TOAD

Animal: Mallorcan Midwife Toad
Class: Amphibia (Amphibian)
Species: *Alytes muletensis*
Status: Vulnerable
Population Trend: Increasing

If you're looking for a species that flips gender roles on their head, look no further than the Mallorcan Midwife Toad! The females of this species compete to mate with available bachelors, and the males carry the babies! And since the males carry the eggs by having a whole string of them wrapped around their ankles, we'd say their gestation period is pretty, uh...*binding*.

These little spotted radicals can only be found on Mallorca, a large island off the coast of Spain. More specifically, they are found up on steep slopes in the Mallorcan mountains and in the gorges of Serra de Tramuntana, where they inhabit pools along the torrents.

From Fossilized to Fully Realized

The Mallorcan Midwife Toad was first discovered in 1977 as a fossil. Everyone figured they had gone Extinct, but two years later, living tadpoles were found! Since then, these froggy folks have met their matches in several other residents of Mallorca. One predator, the Viperine Snake—a non-native species to the island—won't hesitate to gobble them up. And while the larger Green Frog won't eat the Mallorcan Midwife Toad, being in constant competition with them for food gets a little exhausting. Tourism also takes up a lot of the toad's water supply.

Few and Far Between

From a conservation standpoint, the Mallorcan Midwife Toad is one of the most important species in all of Europe. This is mainly because of how few there are and how small and specific their habitat is. There's also evidence that their population used to be a lot bigger. All of this qualifies the Mallorcan Midwife Toad for some of the top wildlife protection measures, including conservation laws at both the state and regional level.

Luckily, these nonconformist toads are basically crushing it as far as species restoration goes! Not only have they mastered breeding in human care, but at least ten populations have been reintroduced into the wild since 1988! Today, conservationists are mainly focused on building new pools for the little froggies since there are still so few options for reintroduction sites.

The Mallorcan Midwife Toad may be classified as Vulnerable, but thanks to the hard work of toad enthusiasts, hopefully they won't be for long!

underfrog ● fact ●

These frogs court each other through various high-pitched "Pi...pi...pi!" sounds.

Male Mallorcan Midwife Toad, carrying eggs, Spain.
Photo © Albert Llea, Minden Pictures

CRAU PLAIN GRASSHOPPER

Animal: Crau Plain Grasshopper
Class: Insecta (Insect)
Species: *Prionotropis rhodanica*
Status: Critically Endangered
Population Trend: Decreasing

There's really no other way to put it—the Crau Plain Grasshopper is an enigma. Little is known about why the southern France native's population has decreased over the last two decades, especially in the Crau steppe, which is a protected area. The camo-colored grasshopper is pretty large—males are about 1.5 inches (31 millimeters), females about 2 inches (45 millimeters)—but that's about where their grasshopper-ness ends. These guys are elusive; they can't fly; they don't really like to sing; and despite being a "grasshopper," they're rather reluctant to hop around on grasses. This is one of the reasons why they can be so hard to find!

The Crau Plain Grasshopper's average life cycle is about forty to forty-six days; they hatch in April, become adults toward the end of May, do the deed, lay eggs, and then live until sometime around July. That's it! In the little time that they do have, the Crau Plain Grasshopper is a total freakin' force when it comes to nutrient cycling. It feeds on a diversity of plants, and then becomes important prey for the birds of the Crau steppe.

At the beginning of the last century, the grasshopper's steppe habitat was partly converted into hay meadow, orchards, farmland, and industrial sites that threatened their survival. Current data points to intensive sheep grazing as the primary threat for the Crau Plain Grasshopper.

And we've got to give it up to the French Army for their commitment to the wild. In 2014, after learning that their project to build a new weapons warehouse threatened the grasshopper's biggest subpopulation, they called off the entire thing and went on to promote the conservation of the species. Talk about an environmental *victoire*.

Who Let the Detection Dogs Out?

In 2014, a new breeding trial was started that produced a ton of eggs and showed some of the first breeding success. As for out in the wild? Conservationists fenced in one small part of the Crau Plain Grasshopper's habitat and saw a significant increase in that population too! And in an innovative twist to try to find more of these easily hidden grasshoppers, researchers have actually begun training detection dogs to find them!

underfrog ●
fact ●

While male Crau Plain Grasshoppers don't have a loud song to attract females like most other grasshoppers do, they do have a loud song that's only produced after mating.

Crau Plain Grasshoppers, Crau Plain, France.
Photo © Axel Hochkirch

BEARDED VULTURE

Animal: Bearded Vulture, aka Lammergeier
Class: Aves (Bird)
Species: *Gypaetus barbatus*
Status: Near Threatened
Population Trend: Decreasing

The Bearded Vulture is probably the most hardcore animal on Earth. First off, it eats bones. And not just the bone marrow, the *entire* bone. It's also known to rub soil and iron oxide from sulfur springs into its feathers, turning them blood red, which some experts believe is actually an intimidation tactic. Numerous fables and legends surround the animal—which is unsurprising, considering it looks like a cross between a phoenix and, well...basically any villain in a sci-fi movie ever. It's even been blamed for the murder of Greek dramatist Aeschylus, who died when a bird, presumed to be the Bearded Vulture, mistook his bald head for a rock and dropped a turtle on it, killing him.

The "Bone-Eater"

Fittingly known in Crete as the "bone-eater," this real-life mythological animal spends its days scavenging for the skeletons of picked-apart carcasses. It swallows small bones whole and breaks bigger ones by dropping them on rocks and flying after them with its signature spiral dive. It has a stomach acid pH of 1, so this raptor is able to digest even the densest of bones in less than twenty-four hours. The thing is also HUGE—it has a wingspan from anywhere between 7 and 9 feet (2–3 meters) and can grow up to 4 feet (1.22 meters) tall!

Raptor Rumors

Back in the 1900s, the Bearded Vulture—also known as the *lammergeier*, which translates to "lamb vulture" in German—was hunted to extinction in many parts of its European range. It didn't actually eat lambs, nor did it eat *children*, like many people believed! Fearing their own kids would be snatched up by a lammergeier, people took to hunting and poisoning the birds, and almost managed to eradicate the entire species from Europe.

Besides being hunted, the Bearded Vulture's other threats include lack of food, eating poisoned baits intended for other predators, and electrocution from colliding with electrical cables and infrastructure.

Bearded Vulture, Valais, Switzerland. Photo © Olivier Born

Nowadays, only about 250 breeding pairs exist in Europe. Thanks to conservationist groups, the Bearded Vulture's image is slowly being rehabilitated, and it's even been reintroduced in the Alps, in Andalusia and Maestrazgo (Spain), and in Grands Causses (France) by the Vulture Conservation Foundation. VCF breeds them in human care and reintroduces them to the area they went Extinct.

underfrog ●
fact ●

The Bearded Vulture is monogamous and only mates once a year.

BELUGA STURGEON

Animal: Beluga Sturgeon
Class: Actinopterygii (Fish)
Species: *Huso huso*
Status: Critically Endangered
Population Trend: Decreasing

Growing as big as 24 feet (7 meters) long and weighing 3,500 pounds (2,000 kilograms), the Beluga Sturgeon is the largest bony fish (fish with skeletons instead of cartilage) in the world. Since they're one of the most primitive lineages of bony fishes, it only makes sense that they look like something straight out of a Jurassic Park movie. They have shark-like tails; hard, bony plates on their sides; and barbels coming out of their snouts that help them locate prey. Sure, the Beluga Sturgeon may look like a huge, terrifying dinosaur, but we assure you, it's completely harmless. And in true introvert form, it actively tries to avoid humans.

A Big Price to Pay

Since it's MASSIVE, the Beluga Sturgeon has few natural predators—however, it was cursed with producing some of the most sought-after caviar in the world: black caviar. Given that a single one of these giant prehistoric catfish-looking animals can produce up to several hundred pounds of black caviar, it is one of the most valuable fish in the world to fisherpeople. This ultimately spells bad news for the species.

What makes matters even worse is that the Beluga Sturgeon is super easy to catch. With a life cycle similar to that of a salmon, it hatches in freshwater rivers, spends its adult life in saltwater oceans, and then goes on to repeat the cycle and spawns upriver. Beluga Sturgeons are most often snatched up in the middle of a spawn.

Nothing to Do but *Ex Situ*

While there have been some events to raise awareness for the Beluga Sturgeon, their only real hope is *ex situ* conservation (taking off-site measures, like conservation breeding programs at zoos and aquariums). This way, the Beluga Sturgeon can ramp up its numbers without having to worry about overfishing and any sort of illegal extractions.

underfrog ●
fact ●

Large sturgeons can live for over one hundred years.

Beluga Sturgeon, Danube Delta Eco-Tourism Museum Centre aquarium, Tulcea, Romania.
Photo © Magnus Lundgren, Wild Wonders of Europe, Nature Picture Library

ROSALIA LONGICORN

Animal: Rosalia Longicorn
Class: Insecta (Insect)
Species: *Rosalia alpina*
Status: Vulnerable
Population Trend: Unspecified

Introducing the Rosalia Longicorn—perhaps the world's most beautiful beetle!

The Rosalia Longicorn is a proud member of the saproxylic beetles, a group of species that depends on dead and decaying wood for the majority of its needs. Like other saproxylic beetles, these fascinating blue beauties do their share of ecosystem work by helping decompose and recycle wood.

Despite flying under the radar, this group of beetles is incredibly important to European habitats. When it comes to dispersing bacteria, fungi, and other organisms, there is truly nothing better than these beetles. They also serve as scrumptious snacks for bats, birds, and other mammals.

In Need of Trees

The Rosalia Longicorn beetles have their own set of struggles. These beauties are listed as Vulnerable, and about 18 percent of saproxylic beetles in Europe are classified as threatened with extinction. Besides having their numbers

decrease, they have to watch as their beloved lifeblood—decaying trees—are logged or dragged away for us to use. Every. Single. Day. Urbanization, tourism development, and agriculture also factor in, and now more than ever, there's an increase in wildfires that often destroy whatever's left.

Growing Forward

If we're talking long-term beetle conservation, the future of this species basically depends on how every generation of trees turns out. In an effort to save the beetles, some urban areas have decided to reduce how many older trees they cut down, and to leave more severed tree trunks open and inhabitable for the little beetles.

As long as their habitats have trees in various states of health—we're talking weaker living trees, dead trees, standing ones, fallen ones, and saplings, all the way up to ancient ones—then and only then can the Rosalia Longicorn finally get comfortable.

Rosalia Longicorn, Vaud, Switzerland. Photo © Olivier Born

underfrog ●
fact ●

Some wood beetles are so picky with their trees that they'll only lay eggs in them if they have a specific hundred-year-old mold growing inside.

MARBLED POLECAT

Animal: Marbled Polecat
Class: Mammalia (Mammal)
Species: *Vormela peregusna*
Status: Vulnerable
Population Trend: Decreasing

Cleverly disguised by an itty-bitty fur "mask," the Marbled Polecat has somehow been able to dodge the limelight it so obviously deserves! With its long, extra-floofy tail, huge ears, and trademark spotted coat, the Marbled Polecat is practically BEGGING to be represented in the form of some kid's stuffed toy. Seriously, just look at it!

Native to southeast Europe (not to mention Turkey, the Middle East, the Caucasus, Iran and Central Asia, northern China, and Mongolia), this precious introvert never ventures far from its home in the steppe. Marbled Polecats have a strong sense of smell, but they do themselves a disservice by releasing foul odors when they feel threatened. In all seriousness, we're sure their skunk-like, uh...*emissions* are quite effective at warding off predators.

A "Steppe" in the Wrong Direction

The biggest threat to the Vulnerable polecat is the loss of their steppe habitats to farmland cultivation. Desertification, which is what happens when fertile land becomes desert due to droughts

and overgrazing, results in another setback: lack of prey for the Marbled Polecat, which can otherwise survive in desert and semidesert habitats. It's also very possible that Marbled Polecats are struggling to find meals since a lot of Europe's steppe rodent species are also decreasing. When they do snatch a meal, they risk getting secondhand rodenticide poisoning.

"Steppes" to Save the Polecat

The Marbled Polecat is protected under the law, making hunting it illegal in most of the countries it lives in. Still, many of the protected areas in the polecat's range are so small that it's proven pretty tough to conserve the species.

Wanting to learn more about the ever-elusive ferret-skunk lovechild, conservationists have made three separate trips to Romania's Dobrogea mountain range, one of the few places where polecats were recorded hanging out in the twentieth century. There, the teams tried out some new research methods—building new tunnels to monitor the polecats, collecting individuals killed on the road, and interviewing local shepherds and farmers. While not a whole lot is known about the day-to-day life of the Marbled Polecat, conservationists are on the right track to figuring out this lanky, wild teddy bear and saving Europe's steppe habitats while they're at it.

underfrog ●
fact ●

The Marbled Polecat is the most fossorial—or most into burrowing—of all weasels.

Marbled Polecat, Stavropol, Russia. Photo © Valeriy Maleev, Nature Picture Library

SOUTHERN CHAMOIS

Animal: Southern Chamois
Class: Mammalia (Mammal)
Species: *Rupicapra pyrenaica*
Status: Least Concern
Population Trend: Increasing

The Southern Chamois (pronounced "shammy" in the United States and "shamuá" in the UK) is a goat-antelope which makes its home up high in the Pyrenees, Cantabrian, and Apennine Mountains. These hook-horned cuties are more sure-footed than even the most experienced hiker—they've been found scaling peaks as high as 9,900 feet (3,000 meters)!

Southern Chamois are generally big on mountain climbing, seasonally migrating in groups or alone from the high-altitude Alpine meadows (their summer home) to steep and rocky wind-protected slopes (their winter home). The chamois is known for its tawny-brown fur and whitish symmetrical face markings that bring to mind the rock band KISS—Gene Simmons, anyone? But the chamois is easiest to identify by the darker band of hair along the sides of its neck that grows in during the winter months. None of the other species of chamois in Central Europe develop this physical trait.

Threats, Threats, and More Threats

Back in the 1940s, the Southern Chamois was hunted for meat and for their skin to make leather. And if you didn't think their leather was enough, the chamois's winter coat was also used to make hats, *and* in some places, their meat was considered a delicacy. Tough break, no? Something else that put a major dent in the chamois's population was a disease called Border Disease Virus, or BDV for short. BDV outbreaks were common in Andorra and the Pyrenees from 2001–2009, and spelled doom for many chamois well into the 2010s.

(continued) ▶

Southern Chamois, Ossau Valley, French Pyrenees.
Photo © Javier Ara

Breeding Programs, Translocations, and Reintroductions, Oh My!

With the Southern Chamois's population back on the up-and-up, there are a bunch of conservation efforts to thank for their survival. A conservation breeding and introduction program has done wonders for the species in Italy, as have translocations in France.

Overall, things are looking pretty good for the Southern Chamois! All the populations of their subspecies are increasing, and since they're all under such tight supervision, an order to ban hunting can be implemented if their numbers ever start to slip. Today, there are about fifty thousand adult Southern Chamois in the world—that ain't too *shammy* if you ask us!

underfrog ●
fact ●

Southern Chamois are proud vegetarians, eating only herbs and flowers and sometimes, though rarely, moss and lichen in the colder months.

LA PALMA GIANT LIZARD

Animal: La Palma Giant Lizard **Status:** Critically Endangered
Class: Reptilia (Reptile) **Population Trend:** Unknown
Species: *Gallotia auaritae* **Last Seen:** 2007 (or earlier)

The La Palma Giant Lizard was—you guessed it—a giant lizard that inhabited La Palma, one of Spain's Canary Islands. Its population started to decrease over two thousand years ago. It has been lost to science since 2007 (if you believe that the photographs published at that time indeed show this species) or for much longer (if you don't). As for the initial demise of this reptilian behemoth, all signs point to the introduction of feral and domestic cats, being hunted by humans, and almost all of the tiny island they live on being converted for agriculture.

If the La Palma Giant Lizard still exists, there likely aren't many of them left. In an interesting turn of events, there have allegedly been a couple sightings on the northern part of the island and some uncon-firmed photographs, like the one in 2007. While this remains unproven, it definitely does give La Palma's reptile fanatics a wild reason to get up in the morning.

Looking ahead, researchers will have to prove whether these sightings are actually of La Palma Giant Lizards. If it turns out they are, they'll have to jump into action immediately to protect the lizard's remaining habitats from agricultural use and prevent anyone from collecting it for food.

So, will the La Palma Giant Lizard ever be found? Stay tuned…

MARIANNE HARTMANN-FURTER

Name: Marianne Hartmann-Furter
European Wildcat Expert
Specialty: European Wildcat Breeding and Conservation
Organization: IUCN SSC Cat Specialist Group

People sometimes give cat ladies a hard time, but Marianne Hartmann-Furter makes being a cat lady—make that a *wild*cat lady—ridiculously cool. Marianne has dedicated herself to saving the European Wildcat, a cute wild floofball who basically looks just like a house cat, but scrappier. A dedicated member of the IUCN SSC Cat Specialist Group, Marianne was the scientific advisor of the European Wildcat reintroduction project in Bavaria, Germany, and has made developing behavior-specific enclosure designs for these wildcats kind of her "thing." At this point, she's basically *the* go-to designer for wildcat, lynx, leopard, and tiger habitats at zoos and wildlife parks. She even started her very own wildcat breeding center in Switzerland!

At Marianne's breeding center, European Wildcat kittens are prepared for reintroduction through limited contact with people, thanks to automated feeders that reduce the constant need for keepers. Besides preparing these kittens for reintroduction, another necessary conservation action is preventing the wildcats from mating with feral domestic cats.

Marianne Hartmann-Furter, European wildcat station, Horgen, Switzerland. Photo © Sigi Weisel

If anyone can make sure this especially adorable species remains as Least Concern, it's badass cat lady Marianne.

PETRA KOVAČ-KONRAD

Name: Dr. Petra Kovač-Konrad
Olm Expert
Specialty: Olm Conservation
Organization: Association Hyla

After graduating from law school, Petra Kovač-Konrad soon realized her heart wasn't actually in the courtroom but in submerged caves!

Eager to learn more about caves and their unique ecosystems, the future conservation hero enrolled in a physical geography and geoecology program and received her PhD in Slovenia. She even wrote her senior thesis on the origin and development of underwater caves.

In 2013, she started working on conserving the Olm in Croatia through Association Hyla. Over the next seven years, Dr. Konrad and her team did more than four hundred dives in these underwater caves, sometimes diving in caves as deep as 4,600 feet (1,400 meters).

On these dives, Dr. Konrad and her team visited up to ten different sites four times per year looking for the Olm. They eventually expanded their deep dives to ten other locations over the years. They took countless photographs and recorded hours of video documentation, wrote a book about the Olm, and gave presentation after presentation on the elusive cave noodle.

Today, Dr. Konrad remains the ultimate example of how important it is to follow your heart, even if it leads you into underwater caves in search of endangered species!

Dr. Petra Kovač-Konrad getting ready to cave-dive in the Spring of Rupecica, Ogulin, Croatia. Photo © Florian Launett, Mala Baka

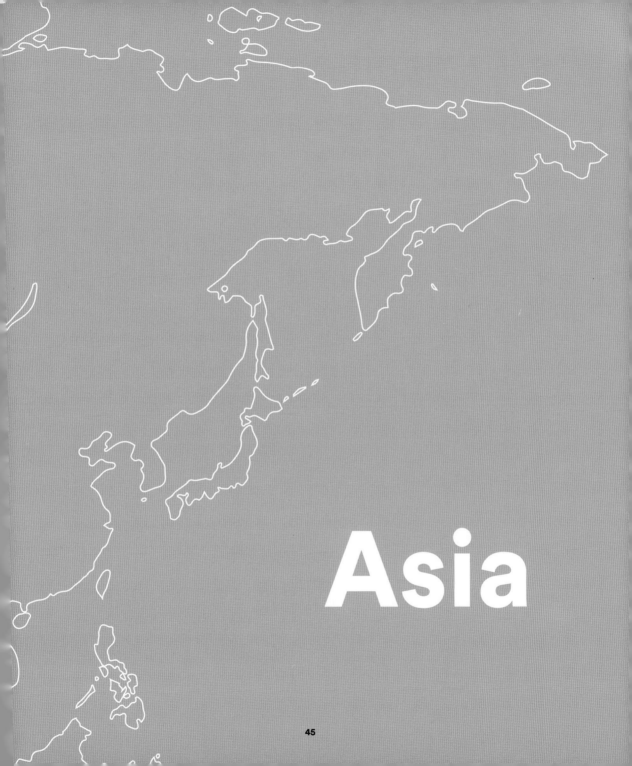

Asia

JAVAN RHINO

Animal: Javan Rhino
Class: Mammalia (Mammal)
Species: *Rhinoceros sondaicus*
Status: Critically Endangered
Population Trend: Stable

A lesser-known cousin of the African rhinos, the Javan Rhino is shy, preferring to spend its days alone, rolling in mud and eating all the twigs, shoots, and fallen fruits its heart desires.

These introverted behemoths stand about 5 feet (1.5 meters) tall at the shoulder and can weigh up to 2 tons (that's 4,000 pounds or 2,000 kilograms!). Their eyesight may not be the best, but their sharp senses of hearing and smell make up for it, helping them find food—and avoid humans at all costs.

The Final Few

The Javan Rhino is one of two rhino species in Indonesia. The last seventy-two Javan Rhinos can only be found in Ujung Kulon National Park on the island of Java. Even there, they are still susceptible to poaching, disease, and natural disasters. Re:wild has partnered with the Rhino Foundation of Indonesia and the International Rhino Foundation in their support of Ujung Kulon National Park to scale up conservation efforts and secure the Javan Rhino population in Ujung Kulon Na-

tional Park. What's the plan? To prevent poaching with badass Rhino Protection Units: four-person teams trained to deactivate traps, apprehend illegal intruders, and investigate crime scenes.

Equally important to the Javan Rhino's long-term success are initiatives to strengthen management of Ujung Kulon National Park; to work with local communities to reduce the spread of disease from domestic cattle into the Javan Rhino herd; to build community support; to maintain and build on a system for monitoring the rhinos; and to establish a second population of Javan Rhinos somewhere not as vulnerable to the threat of tsunamis or volcanic eruptions. (At the moment, a single tsunami or volcanic eruption could wipe out what remains of the entire Javan Rhino species.)

Preventing Poaching

The Javan Rhino has been overhunted for its horns, but fortunately it has been legally protected in Indonesia since 1975. Using mostly foot patrols and camera trap monitoring, park staff

Javan Rhino, Ujung Kulon National Park, Island of Java, Indonesia. Photo © Robin Moore, Re:wild

and conservationists have been able to keep an eye on the species and prevent poaching.

In 2018, Re:wild's very own Dr. Barney Long and Dr. Robin Moore actually got to experience the rare rhino in person, something very few people will ever get to say! Today, the Javan Rhino's numbers are slowly increasing thanks to ongoing conservation measures.

SAOLA

Animal: Saola
Class: Mammalia (Mammal)
Species: *Pseudoryx nghetinhensis*
Status: Critically Endangered
Population Trend: Decreasing

Known as the "Asian unicorn" for its rarity and overall mystical nature, no scientist has actually ever seen the Saola in the wild. We didn't even know it existed until 1992, when one of their skulls was discovered inside a hunter's home in Vietnam.

Both males and females are known for their long, slightly curved horns and unique white face markings. Adults can weigh anywhere from 175 to 220 pounds (80 to 100 kilograms), making the Saola one of the rarest big animals on the planet.

On the Verge

This Critically Endangered species has made its home in the Annamite Mountains of Vietnam and Laos, where it has been hunted to the verge of extinction. Saola—like all other ground-dwelling animals in the Annamite Mountains—are victims of a hunting technique that uses homemade wire snares to catch animals. Snare trapping is so widespread in this region that it has led to what biologists call the "empty forest syndrome."

There are fewer than one hundred Saola left—possibly fewer than twenty. That's a pretty dire number. The good news is that there are many incredible people working to help protect and restore this species.

New Methods, (Hopefully) New Results

Looking toward both immediate and long-term results, Re:wild has partnered with the IUCN SSC Saola Working Group to apply the IUCN's One Plan Approach to save the Saola.

The One Plan Approach is big on the integration of conservation breeding and preservation of animals still living out in the wild. With the help of the governments of Vietnam and Laos, they plan to start a new capture and breeding program in the near future. As a matter of fact, Re:wild is partnering with WWF-Vietnam and Wrocław Zoo to help establish an official conservation breeding facility in Vietnam's Bach Ma National Park to breed and rewild a number of species found in this region, including Saola!

underfrog ●
fact ●

The last time a Saola was seen was on a Worldwide Fund for Nature (WWF)-Vietnam trail camera in 2013.

Saola, Hanoi, Vietnam.
Photo © Toon Fey

TAMARAW

Animal: Tamaraw, aka Philippine Dwarf Buffalo
Class: Mammalia (Mammal)
Species: *Bubalus mindorensis*
Status: Critically Endangered
Population Trend: Decreasing

Have you ever *herd* about WILD cattle?! There are only eleven species of wild cattle left—and the Tamaraw is one of them.

Although its nickname—the Philippine Dwarf Buffalo—certainly fits, this buffalo is one of the larger land mammals in Southeast Asia. At the shoulder, it stands about 4 feet (1.22 meters) tall, which is short in comparison to its other bison-esque cousins. People often note that the Tamaraw's sassy attitude is too big for its smaller stature, kind of like when a Chihuahua barks loudly at a Great Dane. We respect their tenacity, though!

The Pride of a Nation

Rugged. Feisty. Iconic. The Tamaraw is so famous in its part of the world for being tough that Toyota named a pickup truck after it! The Tamaraw is the mascot for the Philippines' Far Eastern University; it has also inspired the names of several sports teams. The animal appears on national currency and postage stamps, and Mindoro Island celebrates Tamaraw month every October.

While at one point there were about ten thousand Tamaraw living on Mindoro Island in the Philippines, that number quickly dropped to around five hundred because of threats like trophy hunting, habitat degradation, and disease. In 1996, a conservation plan was put into action in Mounts Iglit-Baco Natural Park that has since more than doubled the species' population, while Tamaraw populations outside the park drastically decreased or disappeared altogether.

(continued) ▶

Tamaraw in former conservation breeding program, Mindoro, Philippines.
Photo © Daniel Heuclin, Nature Picture Library

In 2018, a team of local, national, and international conservationists, policymakers, and Indigenous peoples (including the Tau-Buid, Buhid, and Alangan communities) developed a plan to continue to bolster these populations, while also reintroducing Tamaraw to two other sites where they were once found. Today, about 80 percent of all Tamaraw live in Mounts Iglit-Baco Natural Park, a tight-knit (but growing) community!

In 2019, Re:wild teamed up with d'Aboville Foundation and Demo Farm Inc. (DAF) and discovered a larger-than-expected population of Tamaraw in remote mountainous areas of Mindoro, outside of Mounts Iglit-Baco Natural Park. This news has continued to spur new hope for the Philippines' national land mammal. The population will help to determine some conservation actions moving forward to recover the species.

underfrog ●
fact ●

The length and thickness of the Tamaraw's horns are good indicators of their age.

TEDDY BEAR PIKA

Animal: Teddy Bear Pika, aka Ili Pika
Class: Mammalia (Mammal)
Species: *Ochotona iliensis*
Status: Endangered
Population Trend: Decreasing

The Ili Pika, the Teddy Bear Pika, the "Magic Bunny," the not-quite Pikachu—any way you put it, this thing is just about as cute as it gets. Rightfully earning all of those names, the Ili Pika is a floofy little mountain dweller that looks part-rabbit and part-feral teddy bear. The Ili Pika was first discovered in China's remote Tianshan Mountains in 1983, where researchers studied it for ten years, recording only twenty-seven individuals during that time. Then the mammal disappeared and was considered lost to science for twenty years until it was spotted again in China's Tianshan Mountains in 2014 by retired conservationist Weidong Li—the very same scientist who originally discovered the species!

Miniature and Mysterious

Not too much is known about the Ili Pika because it lives in such a remote region. We do know they're adorable and quite noticeably anti-social, and that they live in nooks and crannies as high up as 13,450 feet (4,100 meters). They have big rounded furry ears, a black collar, and reddish spots on their muzzle and forehead. They're known to hide in little piles of vegetation—known to pika experts as "haypiles"—that serve as their food sources in the wintertime.

A Sensitive Soul

Another thing about the Ili Pika: They are sensitive to environmental changes. In a 2003 survey of fourteen spots the pikas once called home, only six localities showed any sign that pikas were still living there. More surveys over the

(continued) ▶

next couple of years showed even less evidence of pikas in these places. The exact threats to pikas aren't totally known yet, but scientists chock their notable absence up to increases in sheep grazing and air pollution.

Conservation efforts in place for the little Teddy Bear Pika include protecting their habitat and ongoing education of local people living close to the pika's mountain habitat. Conservationists are hoping all the preciousness of this "Magic Bunny" will help it score some conservation brownie points with the public—another of Mama Nature's little wonderful weirdos that needs to be safeguarded.

underfrog ●
fact ●

Pikas are generally known for their adorable vocalizations, but so far experts haven't heard a peep from the Ili Pika—though they also haven't observed very many to determine whether they actually vocalize.

Teddy Bear Pika, Tianshan mountains, China.
Photo © Weidong Li

FLAT-HEADED CAT

Animal: Flat-Headed Cat
Class: Mammalia (Mammal)
Species: *Prionailurus planiceps*
Status: Endangered
Population Trend: Decreasing

Imagine a house cat. Now imagine if its head was squished a little bit and its eyes were made exponentially bigger. Or imagine a cat was crossed with a bush baby—yeah, that's probably more like it. That's more or less what the Flat-Headed Cat looks like.

One of the rarest small wild cats, there are probably fewer than twenty-five hundred Flat-Headed Cats left in the entire world. These tiny—we're talking 3–5 pounds (1.5–2.5 kilograms) tiny—semiaquatic kitties are extra-un-cat-like thanks to their webbed toes and affinity for water.

Since these cats are so elusive, researchers have had a hard time tracking them down to study them. There are only two Flat-Headed Cats living in human care in the world. Both are at zoos in Malaysia. Besides observing these two, researchers' only other option has been to dive into records of the wild cat dating back to 1984.

For Peat's Sake

Native to the Thai-Malay Peninsula, Borneo, and Sumatra, the biggest threats to the Flat-Headed

Cat are habitat destruction and degradation. (Southeast Asia has the world's highest deforestation rate.) These sweeties mainly live in and around swampy peat bogs—aka the choice place to plant palm oil and establish timber plantations. Sadly, around 70 percent of the Flat-Headed Cat's lowland habitats have already been converted.

Water pollution, a consequence of really gross agricultural runoff and mercury used for gold mining, is also poisoning the fish that the Flat-Headed Cat hunts, which in turn may be poisoning the cats when they eat the fish. Conservation and rewilding initiatives can help reverse this deadly quid pro quo. Restoring the peat bogs the Flat-Headed Cats call home is an important first step.

A Group Effort

Re:wild, Panthera, and the Borneo Nature Foundation are currently working to start a conservation program for the Flat-Headed Cat. In the meantime, the Borneo Nature Founda-

Flat-Headed Cat, Menanggol River, Sabah, Borneo. Photo © Nick Garbutt/www.nickgarbutt.com

tion has zeroed in on peatland restoration and fire control in and around the bogs. Researchers have also continued long-term camera trapping studies to get more photos of the little flat-headed nightstalker. At the rate things are going, we suspect the Flat-Headed Cat could become the poster child for the future of small wild kitty conservation!

underfrog
fact

The Flat-Headed Cat is nocturnal.

SILVER-BACKED CHEVROTAIN

Animal: Silver-Backed Chevrotain
Class: Mammalia (Mammal)
Species: *Tragulus versicolor*
Status: Data Deficient
Population Trend: Decreasing

The Silver-Backed Chevrotain, a tiptoeing, fanged deer-like animal the size of a rabbit, made history in 2019 as the first mammal of our 25 Most Wanted Lost Species to be rediscovered! After planting three trail cameras over the course of five months in southern Vietnam, Re:wild's team finally spotted the less-than-10-pound (4.5-kilogram) animal and took roughly 275 pictures of the little guy. The species was last spotted before that in 1990.

The Small and Species-Confused

Also known as the Vietnamese Mouse-Deer, the Silver-Backed Chevrotain is actually neither a mouse nor a deer—it's the world's smallest hoofed mammal! They are shy and solitary, walk on the tips of their hooves, and can be identified by the silvery sheen on their fur. Oh, and they have two tiny fangs!

Preserving the Lil' Guy

As far as we know, the Silver-Backed Chevrotain can only be found in Vietnam. Sadly, like a lot of the animals in this part of the world, they fall victim to wire snare traps. In an effort to save the chevrotains, Re:wild has successfully continued to survey the animal's home in search of other populations; we also support efforts to prevent poaching in the area they were rediscovered, and are developing a conservation plan to protect and eventually restore the itty-bitty mouse-deer.

At the end of the day, Re:wild's sightings of the Silver-Backed Chevrotain were a testament to the resilience of nature and the importance of our conservation efforts. We hope to have many, many more Silver-Backed Chevrotain sightings in the future!

Silver-Backed Chevrotain, camera trap image, Vietnam.
Photo © Southern Institute of Ecology/Re:wild/Leibniz Institute for Zoo and Wildlife Research/NCNP

underfrog
fact

The Silver-Backed Chevrotain has only been
known to science since 1910.

KLOSS'S GIBBON

Animal: Kloss's Gibbon
Class: Mammalia (Mammal)
Species: *Hylobates klossii*
Status: Endangered
Population Trend: Decreasing

The Kloss's Gibbon is an all-black, tree-swingin', fruit-feedin' monkey you can't help but imagine cuddling. These guys are endemic to Indonesia's four Mentawai Islands: Siberut, Sipora, North Pagai, and South Pagai, which are all just off the west coast of Sumatra. It's in the forests of these islands that the Kloss's Gibbon spends its days swinging from tree to tree and serenading others with its unmistakable—and unimaginably high-pitched—song.

The largest population of Kloss's Gibbons is on the island of Siberut in Siberut National Park, where there are about 10,500 individuals. Sadly, this is nearly a 50 percent population decline since the 1950s. Their total estimated population is around 17,500.

Thanks a Heap, Humans

Since humans arrived on the scene, we have been the only real predator of the Kloss's Gibbons. We hunt them and destroy their home for commercial logging.

Giving the Gibbons a Voice

Recently, an important workshop with key stakeholders resulted in a national strategic action plan for the conservation of the Kloss's Gibbon that outlined some different ways conservationists can help save the gibbon. Some of the ideas thrown around included developing a system to monitor the different populations, starting more awareness programs, and implementing some form of law enforcement in protected areas, including a community-supported investigation network.

underfrog ● fact ●

Some Kloss's Gibbons on Siberut Island produce alarm calls to warn other gibbons of a threat, which can also distract hunters, giving the rest of the group an opportunity to escape.

Kloss's Gibbon, Siberut, Mentawai Islands, Indonesia.
Photo © Arif Setiawan, SWARAOWA

HARVEY'S LICORICE GOURAMI

Animal: Harvey's Licorice Gourami
Class: Actinopterygii (Fish)
Species: *Parosphromenus harveyi*
Status: Endangered
Population Trend: Unknown

No, Harvey's Licorice Gourami isn't a brand of high-end candy—it's a Malaysian freshwater fish. Native to the peat swamps of Peninsular Malaysia, Harvey's Licorice Gourami absolutely craves the dark-colored, highly acidic waters, where it stands out against its murky backdrop.

It's no secret that Harvey's Licorice Gourami is *jaw-droppingly* gorgeous! Its iridescent blue-green accents and fanned tail means this fish stands out in a crowd.

Hit It and Quit It, That's the Motto

This colorful fishy is known for its weird mating ritual. The males court females by pointing their heads downward to show that they're all hot and bothered. Fish enthusiasts call this "flare," similar to a male peacock's love display. As far as the act of copulation goes, let's just say Harvey's Licorice Gourami is here for a good time, not a long time...if you know what we're sayin'. Males and females form temporary bonds to mate, with the responsibility of caring for the eggs falling on the male. (They must have taken a note from the Mallorcan Midwife Toad!)

Getting Bogged Down

Threat-wise, the conversion of peat swamp forests to industrial plantations has done a number on the Harvey's Licorice Gourami. While this fish is still considered common in the peat bogs of northern Selangor, the majority of Malaysia's inhabitable bogs have all dried up, making them unlivable as far as the gourami's standards go. And not only are they found solely in Selangor peat swamp forests; experts also aren't sure the animal could survive in a habitat outside of this home, sweet home. This lack of habitat isn't exactly...uh...*promising* for them. Actually, if we're just looking at habitat destruction, it's projected that Harvey's Licorice Gourami will be Extinct before 2050.

At the moment, there are virtually no conservation efforts in place for this fish. So much is needed: research into its population and day-to-day life, understanding threats to its survival, and monitoring of its well-loved bogs.

underfrog ●
fact ●

Harvey's Licorice Gourami is a micropredator with a picky appetite; the majority of its diet is made up of itty-bitty aquatic invertebrates. As far as these fish are concerned, copepods and mosquito larvae are basically cake!

Harvey's Licorice Gourami, ex situ breeding program, Terengganu, Malaysia.
Photo © Zahar Azuar Zakaria

ANNAMITE STRIPED RABBIT

Animal: Annamite Striped Rabbit
Class: Mammalia (Mammal)
Species: *Nesolagus timminsi*
Status: Endangered
Population Trend: Decreasing

Picture this: A regular rabbit…nothing unusual to see here, just a normal, inconspicuous run-of-the-mill rabbit—but then BOOM! Tiger stripes.

Buckle up, folks. We're talking about the Annamite Striped Rabbit.

Getting its name from the Annamite Mountains on the border of Laos and Vietnam, this bunny was first discovered at a wildlife market there back in 1995 and was described as a new species to science in 2000.

Much of what we know about this elusive animal comes from camera trapping efforts and night surveys across the Annamites. The only quantitative data we have on the species is from a two-year camera trap study conducted in the area. For example, we know that the Annamite Striped Rabbit is strictly nocturnal. We also know that it's mostly solitary and lives in wet evergreen forests. Everything else? Yeah, pretty much a mystery. But we're working on that.

Beware of the Snare

This rare rabbit also faces its fair share of threats. Wire snares—yup, even in protected areas—are probably the biggest culprit of Annamite Striped Rabbit fatalities. (Wire snares are basically the biggest threat to all mammal species living in the Annamite forests.) And of course, we'd be remiss to forget about habitat destruction as the result of extensive logging.

A for Effort (and Also Annamites)

In efforts to conserve the Annamite Striped Rabbit, local governments have teamed up with conservation agencies to form snare trap removal teams. Re:wild partners on these snare removal efforts and also on camera trapping projects across the species' range to understand the status and distribution of the rabbit. Re:wild also hopes to establish a conservation breeding program for the species in the near future.

Annamite Striped Rabbit, Vietnam. Photo © Nikolai Orlov

underfrog ●
fact ●

The Annamite Striped Rabbit's closest evolutionary neighbor—but definitely not their closest geographic neighbor, since they are separated by hundreds of miles of land and sea—is the Sumatran Striped Rabbit, the only other known striped rabbit species in the world.

WALLACE'S GIANT BEE

Animal: Wallace's Giant Bee
Class: Insecta (Insect)
Species: *Megachile pluto*
Status: Vulnerable
Population Trend: Unknown

Let's cut right to it—Wallace's Giant Bee is massive. As far as bees go, that is. Native to the North Molucca islands in Indonesia, this bee has a wingspan of about 2.5 inches (6.35 centimeters) and is roughly four times larger than your average honeybee. (If you need a visual aid, its body is about the size of an adult human thumb.) Let's just say if one of these bad boys flies by your head, you're going to want to duck.

Lost and Found

Wallace's Giant Bee was one of our 25 Most Wanted Lost Species up until it was rediscovered in 2019 and made headlines around the world. Before that, it had been considered lost to science since 1981. On a trip to these remote islands, a team of entomologists and a photographer miraculously found a female giant bee in a termites' nest about 6 feet (2 meters) off the ground! The bees are known to make their homes in the nests of tree-dwelling termites, where they can put their giant jaws to good use and dig into some meaty tree resin. They use the resin to line their nest to defend it and to keep their home dry. These jaws have earned it the harrowing name of the "flying bulldog."

No More Trees = No More Bees

Between 2001 and 2017, Indonesia lost 15 percent of its tree cover to forest destruction for agriculture. Since the giant bee needs lowland forests, it is a goner if all the trees are chopped down. Protections under Indonesian law have been put in place to prevent the collection and sale of the bee.

underfrog ● fact ●

Wallace's Giant Bee can carry marble-sized balls of golden resin with its giant mandibles from nearby trees to its nest.

Wallace's Giant Bee, North Moluccas, Indonesia.
Photo © Clay Bolt

SWINHOE'S SOFTSHELL TURTLE

Animal: Swinhoe's Softshell Turtle, aka Yangtze Giant Softshell Turtle
Class: Reptilia (Reptile)
Species: *Rafetus swinhoei*
Status: Critically Endangered
Population Trend: Unspecified

In Asia, the closest thing to the Loch Ness Monster is Swinhoe's Softshell Turtle. With only four of them left in the world—or, two that are confirmed and two individual turtles that may or may not be Swinhoe's Softshell Turtles specifically—this freshwater-dwelling behemoth is the world's most threatened turtle species. The Swinhoe's Softshell Turtle is one of only two species in its genus, along with its fabulous and also Endangered sibling, the Euphrates Softshell Turtle. All of this to say: Swinhoe's Softshell Turtle is RARE. To make matters worse, one of the last-known female Swinhoe's, XiangXiang, died in 2019. XiangXiang's untimely death made creating more itty-bitty baby Swinhoes a bit harder, we'd say.

A sliver of hope remains—conservationists captured and released one female in a Vietnamese lake after doing a medical checkup. Based on other sightings at this lake and another one, it seems there may be two other Swinhoe's Softshell Turtles in Vietnam, while another, a male, lives in a zoo in China.

A Shell of a Hard Time

How exactly did the Swinhoe's Softshell Turtle dwindle down to such small numbers? To start, they were heavily hunted for more than a century and exploited for food. Everything else can be traced back to wetland destruction, water pollution, and damming of the major rivers they call home.

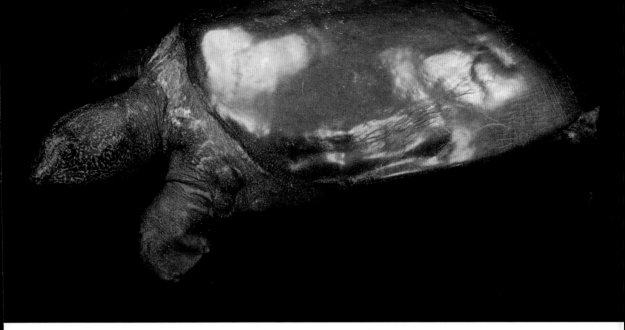

Female Swinhoe's Giant Softshell Turtle, Suzhou Zoo, China. Photo © Joel Sartore/National Geographic Photo Ark

The Dong Mo Lake Lovers

Conservationists are working to build a conservation breeding program for the turtle. The discovery of the female makes this a real possibility. Conservationists from the Asian Turtle Program report another large turtle in Dong Mo and believe it to be a Swinhoe's Softshell also. Hopefully, this means a little population is brewing in Dong Mo Lake!

underfrog ●
fact ●

The Swinhoe's Softshell Turtle can weigh up to 330 pounds (136 kilograms).

MATANG NARROW-MOUTHED FROG

Animal: Matang Narrow-Mouthed Frog, aka Percil Borneo
Class: Amphibia (Amphibian)
Species: *Microhyla nepenthicola*
Status: Least Concern
Population Trend: Decreasing

It's the size of a pea. THIS IS NOT A DRILL. THE MATANG NARROW-MOUTHED FROG IS THE SIZE OF A PEA! Measuring AT MAXIMUM 0.5 inches (1.27 centimeters) long, this frog is *basically* microscopic. It's one of the world's smallest frogs, beaten for the record only by a slightly tinier frog in Cuba. Second place for the title of "smallest frog in the world" is still pretty impressive!

Living on the island of Borneo in Southeast Asia, the majority of these frogs are believed to reside in Kubah National Park. There, the frog is tightly associated with the pitcher plant, its favorite spot for laying eggs. You might think that laying eggs in a carnivorous plant sounds like a bad idea, but for these frogs, it's actually great! The Matang Narrow-Mouthed Frog lays its eggs near the side of the pitcher plant. Once the eggs hatch and become tadpoles, they go hang out in the watery liquid that collects inside the plant. When the babies are big enough (but still very small) they say goodbye to their pitcher plant nursery and venture out into the world!

Shout-Out to Kubah National Park

As it turns out, amphibians are actually the most threatened group of animals in the whole world, which is primarily the fault of a deadly fungal pathogen. More than one-third of amphibians are on the edge of extinction. Luckily, the Matang Narrow-Mouthed Frog isn't one of those. It's currently listed as Least Concern. This is in part because of Kubah National Park, the well-secured and well-managed protected area it lives in.

Matang Narrow-Mouthed Frog, Kubah National Park, Sarawak, Malaysia. Photo © Chien C. Lee

underfrog ●
fact ●

Scientists believe that the Matang Narrow-Mouthed Frog's tiny size
and camouflaged body have long kept it
hidden from researchers.

BALI MYNA

Animal: Bali Myna, aka Bali Starling
Class: Aves (Bird)
Species: *Leucopsar rothschildi*
Status: Critically Endangered
Population Trend: Decreasing

Known for being ridiculously good-looking, the Bali Myna is a white bird with black tips on its wings and tail feathers and cobalt blue skin around its eyes. It's an unmistakable muse for the people of Indonesia, and it even appears in traditional Balinese art.

The Bali Myna was first discovered in 1912 on the north coast of Bali, Indonesia. Because it's so beautiful, the Bali Myna became a major target of the pet trade. In fact, owning one is considered a status symbol in Indonesia.

The Price of Beauty

The mynas are often sold at Indonesia's bird markets, where hundreds of birds are crammed into cages and sold for just one or two dollars. Since Bali Mynas are so gorgeous and so rare, they can usually snag a higher price. This is, sadly, enough of an incentive for poachers to snatch them all up.

Another factor contributing to the myna's steady decline is Bali's hugely successful tourism industry. Bali's human population has tripled within the past seventy years. To top it off, a giant camp for coconut plantation workers was built smack-dab in the middle of a national park the myna called home.

Going International

In the 1960s through the 1970s, the Bali Myna went international—several hundred of them were legally brought to zoos (and went to private collectors) all over the United States and Europe. Today those original birds and their descendants make up around one thousand of the Bali Mynas in the world's zoos. Since not a lot is known about these birds in the wild, the majority of what we do know has come from zoos studying them.

(continued) ▶

Bali Myna, Bali Barat National Park, Bali, Indonesia.
Photo © Ignacio Yúfera, Biosphoto

People have been working to save the Bali Myna by guarding their habitat in West Bali National Park and starting conservation breeding and reintroduction programs. One government-sponsored program even permits locals to bring the birds home on a so-called breeding loan, on one condition: Once the chicklets have grown, the breeder has to give some of them to the park. They are permitted to sell the rest commercially.

A number of nongovernmental organizations (NGOs) are also working together to pull this beautiful bird back from the edge of extinction.

underfrog
fact

The Bali Myna is the official bird of Bali.

LOST SPECIES:
PINK-HEADED DUCK

Animal: Pink-Headed Duck

Class: Aves (Bird)

Species: *Rhodonessa caryophyllacea*

Status: Critically Endangered

Population Trend: Unknown

Last Seen: 1949

Let's be honest: The Pink-Headed Duck was rare to begin with, so it's not *that* shocking that it hasn't been spotted since 1949. This shy, spherical-egg-laying bird once lived all across India, West Bengal, Bangladesh, and Myanmar in the tallest and thickest grasslands and most impenetrable marshes, keeping an extremely low profile. Since then, both hunting and habitat destruction resulted in making an already-rare bird...*rarer*. In 2004, there was an unconfirmed sighting of the duck in a remote Myanmar wetland that reinvigorated the search for it. It then became a race to see who could get the first photograph of the elusive Pink-Headed Duck, but—alas—no one succeeded.

Years later, in 2016, locals from Kachin, the northernmost state of Myanmar, claimed to have spotted the elusive bird, describing it in detail. They told stories of the duck spending time at the marshy and river-crossed area around the vast Indawgyi Lake, far more recently than the last-collected duck in Myanmar, which was way back in 1910.

At Re:wild we're optimistic and continuing the search with partners to find and protect the Pink-Headed Duck. Maybe we'll get lucky with a pink-hued sighting someday soon!

SECTIONOV INOV

Name: Sectionov Inov
Asian Rhino Expert
Title: Program Coordinator (Indonesia)
Organizations: International Rhino Foundation and Rhino Foundation of Indonesia (YABI)

In Sectionov Inov's opinion, the Javan and Sumatran Rhinos are some of the most unique mammals on this planet. And as the International Rhino Foundation's program coordinator for Indonesia, you'd certainly hope he'd think so! Mostly intrigued by the rhino's critical role in its ecosystem, Inov has made it his life's mission to save these great big horned beasts.

Inov started by working with the government of India's Rhino Conservation and soon became a program coordinator in Indonesia for the Rhino Friend Foundation. With RFF, he's planned countless research projects for monitoring, conservation breeding, protection, habitat expansion...you name it, Inov has done it! Most recently, Inov has started partnering with Way Kambas National Park to restore the rhinos' habitat within the park. "We have the on-the-ground experience, strong relationships, and scientific knowledge necessary to protect these Critically Endangered species," Inov says. "Human intervention through partnerships with all stakeholders will be key to protecting these rhinos from extinction."

Sectionov Inov, International Rhino Foundation (YABI) Indonesia coordinator. Photo © The International Rhino Foundation

More than anything, Inov just doesn't want us to be too late to help save the Javan and Sumatran Rhinos. Sure, he's been doing this work for over twenty years now, but Inov knows that there's still a *long* way to go.

ANYA RATNAYAKA

Name: Anya Ratnayaka
Small Wild Cat Expert
Specialty: Small Wild Cat Conservation
Organizations: Urban Fishing Cat Conservation Project,
Small Cat Advocacy and Research, Fishing Cat Conservation Alliance

When it comes to small wild cat conservation, Anya Ratnayaka is our hero! Ever since she stumbled upon Maalu, an orphaned Fishing Cat that was being hand-reared by a vet, Anya's dedicated her time to saving these fluffy, spotted fish-eating fanatics.

After graduating from the University of Queensland in Australia with a degree in wildlife and conservation management, Anya started the Urban Fishing Cat Conservation Project (UFC-CP), which falls under the nonprofit organization she cofounded, Small Cat Advocacy and Research. The project raises awareness of the endangered species and funds research for their team of wild cat lovers. With UFCCP, Anya focuses her research on the only known urban population of Fishing Cats, which have been driven out of their homes in the Sri Lankan wetlands and forced to fend for themselves in the big city.

In an effort to study how these water-obsessed cats adapt to their new *concrete* jungle, Anya and her team at UFCCP launched the first-ever mission to track Fishing Cats with GPS tracking collars. With this technology,

Anya Ratnayaka, cofounder of Small Cat Advocacy and Research.
Photo © Carrie Stengel, Re:wild

Anya can keep watch over the cats, all while collecting information on how we can best protect these amazing animals!

3

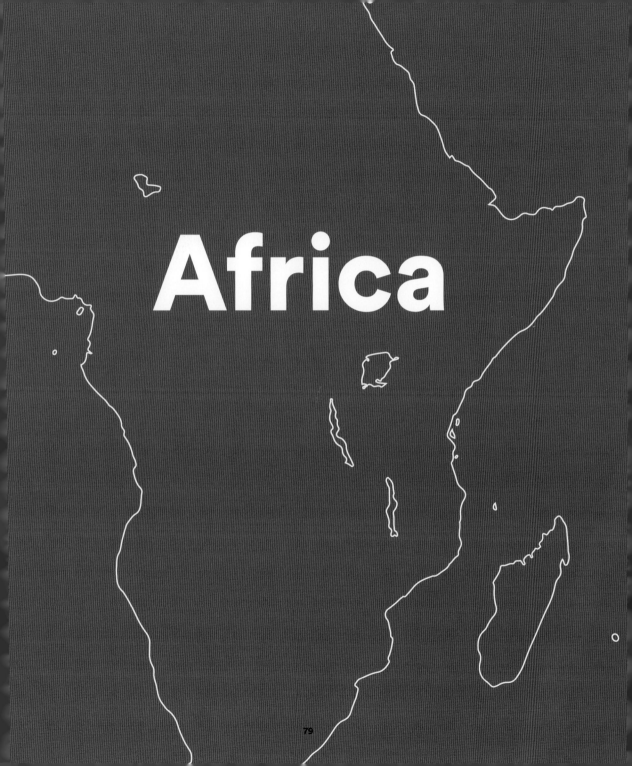

Africa

TEMMINCK'S RED COLOBUS

Animal: Temminck's Red Colobus, aka Temminck's Bay Colobus
Class: Mammalia (Mammal)
Species: *Piliocolobus badius temminckii*
Status: Endangered
Population Trend: Decreasing

If diversity is the spice of life, red colobus monkeys are awfully spicy! They all have different behaviors, vocalizations, and facial expressions, and they even have a wide range of coat colors. They can be blonde, redhead, brunette; grow a beard; go clean-shaven; you name it! Red colobuses are all about variety. They can also live anywhere from Senegal on the Atlantic Ocean to the island of Zanzibar, right off the coast of Tanzania.

One species, Temminck's Red Colobus, has carved out its home range in The Gambia, Guinea-Bissau, Senegal, and Guinea. They act as seed dispersers, toting seeds with them wherever they may go, and keeping their ecosystem fit and fertile! Their stomachs can also ferment leaves and digest plant matter, including plants that other monkeys are unable to digest. It's bon appétit for these vegetarians.

Subpopulations = Susceptible

Of the estimated eighteen distinct forms of red colobus, fourteen of them are listed as either Endangered or Critically Endangered. This makes them the most threatened group of monkeys in mainland Africa. Their future depends on our next moves.

For the Temminck's Red Colobus specifically, habitat destruction is a huge problem. One of their largest populations is in riverine forests around Sambel Kunda in the central river region of The Gambia, where forest cover loss continues to increase. Across West Africa, in fact, more than 80 percent of close canopy forest has been destroyed since 1900. And because of all this habitat destruction and fragmentation, Temminck's Red Colobus populations have been split up into smaller and smaller subpopulations that are more likely to run into people and livestock.

Temminck's Red Colobus is also hunted for bushmeat, and because they don't respond immediately to threats, they are considered easy to catch. They're also the primary prey for chimps. An overall tough break, we'd say.

Communities for Conservation

In 2019, Re:wild began supporting University of Cumbria's Communities for Red Colobus

Family of Temminck's Red Colobus, The Gambia. Photo © Mic Mayhew

Project, aka C4RC. For the project, we zeroed in on two key spots for Temminck's Red Colobus: the Pirang Forest National Park and Sambel Kunda in The Gambia. Our main role is to work as mentors and offer technical advice for the C4RC rangers and community members. Going forward, everyone will be trying to get more people involved on local, national, and international levels.

underfrog ● fact ●

The Temminck's Red Colobus doesn't really have thumbs, just little nubbins.

LOWLAND STREAKED TENREC

Animal: Lowland Streaked Tenrec
Class: Mammalia (Mammal)
Species: *Hemicentetes semispinosus*
Status: Least Concern
Population Trend: Unknown

Legend has it that sometime around sixty million years ago, a small mammal was washed out to sea from Africa on a log or something. This "log" floated all the way to what we know today as Madagascar. And this mysterious little mammal? Well, folks—that was an ancestor of the Lowland Streaked Tenrec.

Today, the Lowland Streaked Tenrec is found only in Madagascar, specifically the forests in the eastern and northern parts of the island. Some might compare the modern-day Lowland Streaked Tenrec to a colorful hedgehog! But even though it does look like a hedgehog-porcupine-anteater lovechild, the tenrec's closest relatives (other than its tenrec cousins in Madagascar) are actually the Otter Shrews.

A Sense-itive Mammal

The Lowland Streaked Tenrec does this cool trick of communicating through different sensory cues. For example, they're big on squeaking and tongue clicking. They also have a patch of quills on their back that form what is called a "stridulating organ." These quills rub together to create a kind of ultrasound that keeps family groups in close contact!

No Worries

Listed as Least Concern on the IUCN Red List of Threatened Species, these guys still have a few things to worry about. Some local villagers hunt them for food, and in most places where they live, their natural forest habitats are being lost to wood harvesting and agriculture. Overall, the Lowland Streaked Tenrec is an extremely adaptable animal who has even been known to reside in some urban areas. They also live in several protected areas, so we'd like to hope things will continue to look pretty good for this little critter.

underfrog ● fact ●

The Lowland Streaked Tenrec loves to burrow, and they're also big on privacy—they often use leaves as "doors" to plug the entrance hole.

Lowland Streaked Tenrec, Masoala National Park, northeast Madagascar.
Photo © Nick Garbutt/www.nickgarbutt.com

RONDO DWARF GALAGO

Animal: Rondo Dwarf Galago
Class: Mammalia (Mammal)
Species: *Paragalago rondoensis*
Status: Critically Endangered
Population Trend: Decreasing

You may know the animals in the genus *Galagos* by their more popular nickname—bush babies! They're easy to obsess over with their big ears, bushy tails, GINORMOUS eyes, and their overall teeny, tiny size. While there are many different types of galagos, the Rondo Dwarf Galago is especially small: weighing in at only around 0.13 pounds (60 grams)! They are one of the world's smallest galago species.

Unlike other galagos, the rare Rondo Dwarf Galago has a tail that looks like a bottle brush. And with their big ol' eyes, it should come as no surprise that these bush babies are nocturnal: Their large eyes help them see in the dark. The Rondo Dwarf Galago spends all day snoozin' away in their treetop nests and make a point to only come out when the moon is up and insects are extra-snackable.

Conserving the Canopy

The Rondo Dwarf Galago makes its home in coastal Tanzania, where agricultural encroachment, charcoal manufacturing, and logging are the main causes of destruction to the galago's habitat. This is terrible for the bush baby because it makes its home in the forest canopy. And since these galagos already live in small, fragmented populations, habitat loss only drives groups farther and farther apart.

Standing Up for the Lil' Guy

And now for some good news! Conservationists have launched several initiatives to protect the Rondo Dwarf Galago, including efforts to lessen land conflicts between the forest management authorities and the local communities, and the enforcement of all protected area laws and policies. They've also made a point to get out in the field and learn more about the Rondo Dwarf Galago's presence and population distribution. With a team of conservationists on their side, we hope the Rondo Dwarf Galago isn't Critically Endangered for much longer. Fingers, toes, and bottle-brush tails crossed!

Rondo Dwarf Galago, Noto Plateau Village Forest Reserve, Tanzania. Photo © Andrew Perkin

underfrog ●
fact ●

The Rondo Dwarf Galago is known for its unique "double unit rolling call," which consists of two soft chirps, starting with one higher in pitch. They repeat this over and over like a song when they emerge at dusk.

HIROLA

Animal: Hirola
Class: Mammalia (Mammal)
Species: *Beatragus hunteri*
Status: Critically Endangered
Population Trend: Decreasing

As the last remaining member of its genus, the Hirola is probably just about the rarest and most endangered antelope out there. Its population has declined by more than 95 percent in the last four decades. If it does go Extinct, the Hirola would be the first Extinct genus on the African continent since the evolution of modern humans.

Hirola live in southeast Kenya and possibly southwest Somalia. Tragically, a lot of their Somalian population has been chased out by civil and military conflicts in the area and has been subsequently lost or displaced.

Only Five Hundred Left

Currently, there are about five hundred Hirola left in the world. This massive decline in numbers was caused first by a disease that knocked them down to low numbers. Then the loss of elephants from their shared landscape resulted in an increase in tree cover and invasive grasses, which means lower-quality food for the Hirola and easier hunting (of Hirola) by lions.

(continued) ▶

Hirola, Tsavo East National Park, Kenya.
Photo © Robin Moore, Re:wild

A Future for the Hirola

Re:wild has partnerships with several organizations that are completely gung ho about Hirolas. They are the Hirola Conservation Program (focused on improving grazing and area-wide protection), Northern Rangelands Trust (supporting predator-proof fencing and community conservation), and the Tsavo Trust (which is *all* over monitoring). Together, these organizations make a pretty incredible team. With all our bases covered, a future for the Hirola finally doesn't seem all that out of reach!

underfrog ●
fact ●

Hirola have dark glands under their eyes that emit pheromone-containing secretions, which they use to mark their territories. These glands earned them the nickname "the four-eyed antelope."

VERREAUX'S SIFAKA

Animal: Verreaux's Sifaka
Class: Mammalia (Mammal)
Species: *Propithecus verreauxi*
Status: Critically Endangered
Population Trend: Decreasing

They can be found up in the highest of canopies or down on the ground sashaying like kids at a dance recital—we're talking about the Verreaux's Sifaka! These guys are often called the "Dancing Verreaux's Sifaka" because of their bouncy, dance-like way of moving. In fact, they can easily clear *30 feet* (9 meters) in one bound! This white lemur is only found in Madagascar, specifically in its southwestern dry lowland and mountainy forests. These lemurs have become basically synonymous with Madagascar, attracting tourists from all over the world. Not a lot of people know this, but lemurs are actually the most endangered group of primates in the world. Out of the 111 lemur species and subspecies that exist, about 95 percent of them are threatened with extinction. The Verreaux's Sifaka is no exception.

Home-Not-So-Sweet-Home

Threat-wise, these dancing lemurs have a lot of forces working against them. Slash-and-burn agriculture, logging, charcoal production, savanna fires, and climate change have all done a number on their habitat. Recently, experts have also come to believe that a parasite or some sort of tick-borne disease is playing a role in the Verreaux's Sifaka's more sudden decline. Demand for lemurs in the exotic pet trade is also on the rise.

(continued) ▶

Protected Areas That Aren't All That Protected

Verreaux's Sifakas live in a number of different national parks, wildlife reserves, and large protected areas, but they need more than space in parks and reserves to keep them safe; they need guardians to protect them from being hunted. Human population growth is also starting to close in on these spots.

Let's put it this way: Lemurs are to Madagascar what pandas are to China. They're cute! They're iconic! Every little kid wants a stuffed animal toy of them! If we don't step up to help the Verreaux's Sifaka, they could be gone before we know it. And we don't know about you, but we think the world could use some more dancing lemurs.

underfrog ● fact ●

Like other sifakas, the Verreaux's Sifaka uses its long tail for balance when moving between trees and raises its arms to keep its balance when it "dances."

Verreaux's Sifaka, privately owned wildlife reserve of Berenty, Toliara, Madagascar.
Photo © Chien C. Lee

GEOMETRIC TORTOISE

Animal: Geometric Tortoise
Class: Reptilia (Reptile)
Species: *Psammobates geometricus*
Status: Critically Endangered
Population Trend: Decreasing

Called the "Fabergé egg" of tortoises, the Geometric Tortoise is easily identifiable by the—can you guess? That's right, the geometric pattern on this tortoise's shell gives it away every time. Unlike the tortoises we're all a little more familiar with, which can live for over one hundred years, the Geometric Tortoise's life span generally caps off at around forty years. And while some tortoises may be absolutely *giant*, the Geometric Tortoise only grows to be 5–6 inches (13–15 centimeters) max!

90 Percent Homeless

Living only in South Africa's Western Cape, this little tortoise lost more than 90 percent of its natural habitat to agriculture. Its original habitat has been converted into vineyards, fruit orchards, and wheat fields. With only around one thousand individuals left in the wild, the Geometric Tortoise has unfortunately solidified its standing among the world's most endangered tortoises and freshwater turtles.

Guarding the Geometric Tortoise Preserve

Re:wild, along with several other conservation groups, has partnered with the Turtle Conservancy in South Africa. Together, we purchased 865 acres (3.5 square kilometers) of the last remaining Geometric Tortoise habitat and have named this land the Geometric Tortoise Preserve. There, a guardian team spends their time taking care of the land and looking after the tiny tortoises. These guardians receive training in habitat restoration, and work to clear invasive plant species, build fences, route irrigation, and install firebreaks.

underfrog ●
fact ●

The Geometric Tortoise is one of the rarest tortoises in the world. Trading them is illegal under international law, which means you won't find any in your local pet stores.

Geometric Tortoise, Geometric Tortoise Preserve, the Western Cape of South Africa.
Photo © Dewald Kirsten Photography

PLOUGHSHARE TORTOISE

Animal: Ploughshare Tortoise, aka Angonoka
Class: Reptilia (Reptile)
Species: *Astrochelys yniphora*
Status: Critically Endangered
Population Trend: Decreasing

Say *shello* to the Ploughshare Tortoise—a show-stopper if we've ever seen one. Like other victims of poaching and the exotic pet trade, the Ploughshare Tortoise pays an unfortunate price for its good looks: It is Critically Endangered.

It's thought that fewer than two hundred adult ploughshares remain in the wild today. The "wild" that we're talking about here is strictly the Baly Bay region of Madagascar. In this small area, the last remaining Ploughshare Tortoises pass the hours sitting, snoozing, or snacking on herbs, grasses, and shrubs. The males also consider themselves wrestlers—they compete for females through "wrestling" matches, using the plow-shaped front part of their shells to try to flip their opponent over.

The Ploughshares' Saviors

To prevent the Ploughshare Tortoise from being poached for the international pet trade, Re:wild's partners, Durrell Wildlife Conservation Trust and the Turtle Conservancy, have really stepped up security measures for the last of the wild populations. The tortoises are protected with guards, razor wire, and even some hidden cameras to keep an eye out for poachers.

Conservationists are also creating new breeding colonies to help reduce overcrowding and theft in one *very* successful breeding facility! Other ongoing efforts include finding and rescuing Ploughshare Tortoises that have been trafficked into the pet trade. When a tortoise is found, it is added to breeding groups and prepared for reintroduction.

underfrog fact

When kept in human care, male Ploughshare Tortoises have to be separated from one another because they'll try to beat each other up. (It's a dominance thing.)

Ploughshare Tortoise, Baie de Baly National Park, Madagascar. Photo © James Liu, Turtle Conservancy

GOLIATH FROG

Animal: Goliath Frog, aka Giant Slippery Frog
Class: Amphibia (Amphibian)
Species: *Conraua goliath*
Status: Endangered
Population Trend: Decreasing

The Goliath Frog is the largest frog species in the world. Like, it's huge—the thing can weigh up to *8 pounds* (3.63 kilograms). It seems as though these gargantuan amphibians know they're big. The frogs use their size to move rocks to create little ponds for females to lay their eggs in. (Scientists believe that building these physically demanding nests is probably one of the reasons these guys evolved to be so huge.) When it comes to mating, the Goliath Frog lacks vocal sacs, so it had to come up with new, alternative ways to attract the hotties. Adaptable as always, the Goliath Frog holds his mouth open and whistles to find a mate.

A Prime Population Regulator

These absolute loaves of frogs are found in southwest Cameroon and Equatorial Guinea, where they help regulate other populations via their healthy appetite for insects, fish, little mammals, and other amphibians. In this way, the Goliath Frog helps make sure that rainforest river habitats don't become overpopulated.

A Delicate Delicacy

In Cameroon, the locals consider the Goliath Frog a culinary delicacy. This demand for them has done a number on their population. Habitat destruction has also played a role in their decline; a majority of their favorite spots have been converted into farmland.

Next Steps?

The Goliath Frog is thought to live in a number of protected areas, including Monte Alen National Park in Equatorial Guinea. Right now, there are not many conservation efforts in place to help protect them. The next steps, according to experts, are to implement some conservation breeding programs and work with locals to regulate the harvesting of the Goliath Frog at more sustainable levels.

underfrog ● fact ●

Goliath Frogs aren't just big; they can jump almost 10 feet (3 meters)! In addition, their tadpoles are super picky eaters. They eat just one species of plant found near waterfalls and the banks of rivers.

Goliath Frog, Cameroon.
Photo © Cyril Ruoso, Nature Picture Library

MALAGASY GIANT JUMPING RAT

Animal: Malagasy Giant Jumping Rat

Class: Mammalia (Mammal)

Species: *Hypogeomys antimena*

Status: Endangered

Population Trend: Unknown

The Malagasy Giant Jumping Rat has claimed the title of the biggest rodent in all of Madagascar. The jumping rats live in the Menabe Antimena forest, which is a protected area, but the widespread illegal destruction of the dry forest inside the park boundaries is a serious threat to the species. Being nocturnal, they spend all night foraging around the forest floor for fallen fruit, seeds, and leaves. They also LOVE to burrow and are known to dig tunnels as deep as 16 feet (5 meters) with six different entrances to their subterranean estates!

'Til Death Do They Part

The Malagasy Giant Jumping Rat mates for life. You might be wondering: What happens if one dies? In the case of a fatality, females stay inside their burrow until a new mate comes their way. Males usually do the same, but sometimes they've been known to move in with a widowed rat.

Save That (Jumping) Rat!

Living in Madagascar, the Malagasy Giant Jumping Rat constantly has to worry about losing its dry forest home to make room for slash-and-burn agriculture, charcoal production, and timber. A road was recently constructed that cuts right through their range, and this has essentially split their habitat in half.

But in 2006, the amazing Durrell Wildlife Conservation Trust stepped up to help this Endangered R.O.U.S. (Rodent of Unusual Size). They've been able to capture the first-ever trail camera footage of the species, to start a conservation breeding program, and to set up special community control teams to help stop illegal activities such as deforestation in the national park. Durrell Wildlife Conservation Trust has also successfully recruited other organizations to help protect these rat kings.

underfrog ●
fact ●

Female jumping rats can give birth twice in one single reproductive period. Wild, right?!

Malagasy Giant Jumping Rat, Jersey Zoo, Jersey.
Photo © Gregory Guida, Durrell Wildlife Conservation Trust

WHITE-BELLIED PANGOLIN

Animal: White-Bellied Pangolin, aka African Tree Pangolin
Class: Mammalia (Mammal)
Species: *Phataginus tricuspis*
Status: Endangered
Population Trend: Decreasing

Protected by an impenetrable coat of scales, the White-Bellied Pangolin looks like Africa's knight in shining armor. It may resort to rolling up into a ball when it feels even the *slightest* bit threatened, but in our eyes, it's still nothing short of a hero! Pangolins are the world's only scale-covered mammals, and their scales are made of the same material that makes up your fingernails: keratin.

The White-Bellied Pangolin gets its name—this may shock you—from its white underbelly. They are also the smallest pangolin species (between 6.6 and 12.2 pounds [3 and 6 kilograms]), the size of a small house cat, and have three-pointed scales, which are unique among the eight pangolin species.

Another physical feature we can't forget about is their prehensile tail. This strong and flexible appendage can curl around and grasp tree branches and essentially works as a fifth limb. This makes the White-Bellied Pangolin an expert tree climber, which helps them search for their favorite food—ants!

Trafficked for Trade

All eight species of pangolins have scaly armor tough enough to protect them from lions, yet that's not enough to protect them from their top predator: humans. Pangolins are estimated to be the most trafficked mammals in the world. Even though they are listed under wildlife protection laws, they're still constantly hunted for their scales (which are used in traditional medicines, though they have no proven medicinal value) and their meat (which is considered a delicacy in East Asia).

Protecting the Pangolin

Some of the leading groups working to protect pangolins are Save Pangolins, Pangolin Crisis Fund, and the IUCN SSC Pangolin Specialist Group. The world's governments are also taking action to help save pangolins. More than 180 countries agreed in 2016 that pangolins are so threatened that they are at serious risk of extinction. International commercial trade of the scaly mammals was subsequently banned. But criminal networks are still trading pangolins illegally, and much work still needs to be done.

Experts say that the next steps need to be making sure pangolins are safe from hunting in the wild places where they live. At the rate things are going, White-Bellied Pangolins are being hunted *much* faster than the animal is able to reproduce. This time, it's the knight in shining armor's turn to be rescued.

underfrog ● fact ●

The White-Bellied Pangolin is still the one you're most likely to run into in the wilds of Central and West Africa—except they like to hang out in trees, making a pangolin sighting rare!

White-Bellied Pangolin, Odzala-Kokoua National Park, Republic of the Congo.
Photo © Jabruson, Nature Picture Library

NORTHERN BALD IBIS

Animal: Northern Bald Ibis
Class: Aves (Bird)
Species: *Geronticus eremita*
Status: Endangered
Population Trend: Stable

The Northern Bald Ibis has such an intimidating appearance, with its long beak, bald head, and beautiful green-black iridescent plumage that ancient Egyptians believed it was a divinity of the underworld.

Also called the Waldrapp, this strange and magnificent species likes to nest up in dry, rocky areas like cliffs. Further capitalizing on its villainous, dark lord–demigod image, the Northern Bald Ibis is also known to inhabit old decrepit castles, walls, and ruins. Very on-brand!

Not Much of a Looker

Even with its once-presumed sacred afterlife ties, the Northern Bald Ibis is still one of the most threatened birds in the world. Why? Many think it's because this bird is a little bit spooky-looking. The Northern Bald Ibis used to exist all across northern Africa, West Asia, Arabia, and Central Europe. Now, almost all of the wild birds live in one specific subpopulation in Morocco, and there might still be a tiny group of them in Syria too.

How did the Northern Bald Ibis become Endangered? It's not entirely clear what caused a decline in the populations historically, but today the bird faces a number of threats, including poaching, habitat destruction and degradation, and pesticides.

Conservation Innovation

On the subject of conservation, some pretty cool stuff is happening for the Northern Bald Ibis. Wardens provide safe, fresh water for the Moroccan wild colonies, which helps improve their reproductive success. There are also efforts to guide the birds via microlites (or ultralight aircraft) across the Alps to Italy. Other efforts are still being perfected and could be useful in the bird's former range. For example, a team in Germany took to the skies—quite literally—in the name of survival! This innovative effort involved a team raising a whole flock of ibis from birth and then guiding them out into the wild via a paramotor (kind of like a paraglider but with a motor!). This helped the birds relearn old migration routes.

underfrog ●
fact ●

The Northern Bald Ibis's likeness has appeared in Egyptian hieroglyphs that date back thousands and thousands of years.

Northern Bald Ibis, Tamri, Morocco.
Photo © Bruno D'Amicis

PINSTRIPE DAMBA

Animal: Pinstripe Damba
Class: Actinopterygii (Fish)
Species: *Paretroplus menarambo*
Status: Critically Endangered
Population Trend: Unknown

The bluish, grayish, reddish Pinstripe Damba, with their red tails for which they are named (*menarambo* means "red tail" in Malagasy), were discovered in Lake Sarodrano in Madagascar in the early 1990s. But—almost like something out of a true-crime show—the Pinstripe Damba vanished shortly after it was first seen. It wasn't until 2006 that it was rediscovered in nearby Lake Tseny.

A lot about the Pinstripe Damba still remains a mystery. What we do know, however, is that they're all about the sort of "underwater forests" these lakes provide, and they like to swim through the vegetation and use it as cover. They almost exclusively feed on small gastropods (snails and slugs). The Pinstripe Damba is also threatened by overfishing.

Plus One for the Zoos

These days, overfishing is still an issue for the Pinstripe Damba, coupled with habitat degradation and some newfound invasive species that have decided to join the party in Lake Tseny. Luckily, though, conservation breeding groups in the United States and Europe are ensuring the survival of the species, all while teaching conservationists more and more about this fish.

One of the places breeding the Pinstripe Damba is the ZSL Whipsnade Zoo in England. ZSL Whipsnade Zoo has managed to replicate the habitats of many endangered aquatic species, including that of the Pinstripe Damba. Zurich Zoo in Germany also has several dambas and continues to study them every day.

(continued) ▶

Pinstripe Damba, ZSL Whipsnade Zoo, England.
Photo © Jack Perks Wildlife Media

A Literal Fish Festival

Local conservationists in Madagascar are *definitely* not sleeping on the Pinstripe Damba rescue efforts either. Awareness campaigns have been popping up for the fish—posters using the local dialect have been put up all around Lake Tseny, it's been discussed by experts on local radio shows, and there was even a *festival* to mark the end of the fishing season! Some fishing regulations have also been put into place, like only using specific net mesh sizes so that juveniles can escape them and go on to grow up and reproduce. Closing the fishing season—with a festival, no less—also gives the Pinstripe Damba more time to breed, produce, and develop. We'd say that's a pretty great reason to celebrate!

underfrog ● fact ●

Before it went Extinct in Lake Sarodrano, the Pinstripe Damba was considered an important food fish within its ecosystem.

LOST SPECIES:
TOGO MOUSE

Animal: Togo Mouse, aka Groove-Toothed Forest Mouse, Buettner's Togo Mouse
Class: Mammalia (Mammal)
Species: *Leimacomys buettneri*

Status: Data Deficient
Population Trend: Unknown
Last Seen: 1890

The Togo Mouse was first discovered in 1890 and *supposedly* hasn't been seen since. But it's a tiny mouse...it could be pretty easy to overlook, right?

The two individuals that were found were discovered in unknown habitat, and their teeth and stomach contents suggested that they were insect eaters. It's even possible that they came from open-country landscape rather than rainforest, because their Latin name is derived from a Greek word that means "meadow" or "garden." Besides this, not much else is known about the possibly Extinct—or just inspiringly elusive—critter. The original two individuals were the only ones to ever be recorded by Western scientists.

In 1990, some scientists were bit by the Togo Mouse bug and launched two different expeditions to rediscover the species. Sadly, neither trip uncovered any sort of mousy evidence. What's curious, though, is that years later, some interviews with Ghanaian hunters suggested that locals had seen the mouse as recently as 2011. The same thing happened with the field staff of Kyabobo National Park, who recognized the Togo Mouse when they were shown photos. According to these locals, they even gave it a name, "Yefuli." This makes us pretty optimistic that the Togo Mouse is still out there doing what it does best!

MISS WALDRON'S RED COLOBUS

Animal: Miss Waldron's Red Colobus
Class: Mammalia (Mammal)
Species: *Piliocolobus waldroni*

Status: Critically Endangered
Population Trend: Decreasing
Last Seen: Côte d'Ivoire in 1978

Nobody has seen Miss Waldron's Red Colobus in almost forty-five years. If this species is confirmed to be Extinct, it will be the first recorded primate species extinction in five hundred years.

Miss Waldron's Red Colobus is a red and black monkey native to western Ghana and eastern Côte d'Ivoire. It became known to science for the first time in 1933, when a British museum collector found it and named it after a colleague on the same expedition: Miss F. Waldron.

Excitement over the discovery was short-lived. Except for evidence from a hunter, who had a skin believed to belong to a red colobus, which suggested a small group of these monkeys might still exist in the southeast corner of Côte d'Ivoire, Miss Waldron's Red Colobus wasn't seen again until 1978—forty-five years later.

Since then, conservationists have set up camera traps hoping to catch a glimpse of this primate, with little luck. Re:wild has even helped set up the Red Colobus Working Group along with the African Primatological Society and IUCN SSC Primate Specialist Group to conduct some range-wide protection efforts. Hopefully with all this, it won't be another forty-five years until Miss Waldron's Red Colobus shows up!

LOST SPECIES:
ST. HELENA DARTER

Animal: St. Helena Darter

Class: Insecta (Insect)

Species: *Sympetrum dilatatum*

Status: Critically Endangered

Population Trend: Unknown

Last Seen: 1963

St. Helena is a *tiny* Overseas Territory of the United Kingdom that's found in the South Atlantic Ocean. The small island is rich with wildlife, including 420 species of invertebrates that are found nowhere else in the world. One of these species—which has been lost to science since 1963—is the St. Helena Darter. The St. Helena Darter is a huge, vibrant, bright red dragonfly. In fact, it has especially large wings for a darter, at over 2.75 inches (7 centimeters). The St. Helena Darter is only one of these incredible-yet-lost species, which also include the Giant Ground Beetle and the Giant Earwig, the largest earwig ever found on Earth (even earwig fossils aren't as big!).

All of these species lived together on the island blissfully until about five hundred years ago when we humans showed up. Since then, there's been a steady stream of extinctions.

However, it's not all bad news. A dedicated bunch of conservationists have fallen in love with this bizarrely biodiverse island and its amazing endemic invertebrates. Today, the St. Helena National Trust and the IUCN Mid-Atlantic Islands Invertebrate Specialist Group are working hard to preserve and even bring back some of the island's weird and wonderful invertebrates. We hope we'll see some of these wonderful insects again sometime soon!

RACHEL ASHEGBOFE IKEMEH

Name: Rachel Ashegbofe Ikemeh
Red Colobus Expert
Organization: Southwest Niger Delta Forest Project

When talking about red colobus monkeys, we'd be remiss not to mention Rachel Ashegbofe Ikemeh, queen of all things colobus! This gal isn't afraid to trudge through waist-deep water to get to the forest swamps where these monkeys live—in fact, there's nowhere else she'd rather be!

Rachel currently serves as the director of the Southwest Niger Delta Forest Project, where she works tirelessly to preserve the wildlife in the southwest and Niger Delta of Nigeria. For example, over the course of seven years, Rachel worked with the Apoi community in Nigeria to start a community conservancy for the Niger Delta Red Colobus. (This is only the second community conservancy in all of Nigeria.)

Also, because of the impact of her work on chimpanzees, Rachel was awarded a Whitley

Rachel Ashegbofe Ikemeh, director of the Southwest Niger Delta Forest Project.
Photo © Kosiprey William, SW/Niger Delta Forest Project

Award in 2020—and if you're not familiar with the Whitleys, let's just say they're basically the "green Oscars."

BADRU "MWEZI" MUGERWA

Name: Badru "Mwezi" Mugerwa
African Golden Cat Expert
Organization: Embaka-Saving African Golden Cats

Badru Mugerwa isn't your average city boy. Born in Kampala, Uganda, Badru has since ditched the city lights for a more unpredictable life out in the wild. Today, he's the founder of Embaka, a community-based conservation initiative that works with local Ugandan communities to prevent poaching, a serious threat to the African Golden Cat. Embaka provides services such as free oral healthcare and improving local household income for the folks who live in the remote areas on the frontlines of African Golden Cat habitats, in return for their help with anti-poaching efforts. Former poachers have been so moved by Badru's work that they have joined Embaka. Pretty incredible, right?

In his own words, Badru says Embaka "focuses on the interactions between people and biodiversity." This approach to conservation has solidified Badru's spot as a rising conservation star. He's recently been named president-elect of the Society for Conservation Biology's Africa section, as well as the International Congress for Conservation Biology's chair for its steering committee. We can't wait to see what Badru and Embaka accomplish next!

Badru Mugerwa, founder of Embaka, sets a camera trap in Uganda.
Photo © Benjamin Drummond

North America

JAMAICAN IGUANA

Animal: Jamaican Iguana
Class: Reptilia (Reptile)
Species: *Cyclura collei*
Status: Critically Endangered
Population Trend: Unknown

If you want to hear about an ongoing conservation success story, then we need to talk about the Jamaican Iguana! Though this lizard disappeared in the early 1950s, it was fortuitously rediscovered in the Hellshire Hills on Jamaica's mainland in 1990. The ashy blue and gray iguana is a real stunner, complete with red eyes. They also have lovely triangular designs on their backs just for some added chevron flair!

A Forty-Year Hiatus

What caused these gorgeous reptiles to decline so much? Scientists believe it all goes back to the late 1800s, when certain non-native mammals—mainly mongooses and feral pigs—were introduced to the island. The baby Jamaican Iguanas quickly became the prey of the mongooses and the feral pigs.

Another big threat to the Jamaican Iguana's survival is the charcoal industry. The charcoal industry relies on hardwood trees that grow in Hellshire Hills, so when those are cut down and harvested, the iguana's habitat is totally obliterated.

We Wanna Save the Iguana!

Here's the good news, though: There was supposed to be this giant transshipment port built on Jamaica's Goat Islands, but Re:wild and Jamaica Environment Trust joined forces with local communities and other partners to help stop it, in part by bringing international attention to the threat. Today, instead of hosting a transshipment port, the island is now set to be part of a protected area! This is a huge win for all the local species, but mostly for the Jamaican Iguana.

The next step to save the Jamaican Iguana and expand reintroduction efforts is to release a bunch of young iguanas, raised in human care, out onto Goat Islands once all the invasive species have been removed, so they can live out their free, uninhibited lives. Other organizations are leading the charge to save this species, including the International Iguana Foundation and Hope Zoo in Kingston, Jamaica, which started the Jamaican Iguana Head Start Program to provide health screenings for iguanas that are ready to be released. The Urban Development Corporation (UDC) and the National Environment & Planning Agency (NEPA) even signed an official memorandum protecting the Goat Islands. Thanks to this massive group effort, the Jamaican Iguana should soon get to enjoy its predator-free island!

**underfrog ●
fact ●**

Female Jamaican Iguanas can lose up to half of their entire body weight after laying their eggs!

Jamaican Iguana, Hellshire Hills, Jamaica.
Photo © Robin Moore, Re:wild

CUBAN CROCODILE

Animal: Cuban Crocodile
Class: Reptilia (Reptile)
Species: *Crocodylus rhombifer*
Status: Critically Endangered
Population Trend: Unspecified

Imagine you're in a lush remote part of Cuba—more specifically, the Zapata Swamp, Cuba's largest coastal wetland. You turn to your left, and there it is: the Cuban Crocodile, in all of its over-10-foot (3-meter) glory! These black and yellow crocs are awe-inspiring predators. They're strong swimmers and are also good at getting around on land, so, to put it simply, no small mammal is safe. The Cuban Crocodile's hind legs are super strong, and the reptile uses tail thrusts to leap from the water, snatching birds and other prey from overhanging branches. This is one powerful animal!

These Critically Endangered ancient reptiles also have a reputation for being curious. So curious, in fact, that they've been known to wander onto campsites in search of warm places to sleep. Waking up to a 10-foot-long reptile underneath your hammock would be pretty cool, right?...*right?!*

Hybridizations from Different Nations

Illegal hunting has put a wrench in the Cuban Crocodile population. That, and their hybridization with American Crocodiles. (Hybridization occurs when one species breeds with another.) This cross-croc hybridization happens because Cuban Crocodiles have been pushed farther into the coastal habitats of American Crocodiles to avoid being hunted for their skins and to escape the destruction of their swampy habitats. But if the two species continue to interbreed, there won't be any Cuban Crocodile genetics left.

Swampy Saviors

Luckily for the Cuban Crocodile, they have the Zapata Swamp Captive Breeding Farm, the most luxurious croc rehab facility! Here they breed and release the crocodiles, and have outreach programs that work to reduce poaching and the consumption of crocodile meat. All in all, the Zapata Swamp Captive Breeding Farm, in partnership with the Wildlife Conservation Society, is making strides in helping rewild this reptile.

Cuban Crocodile at a crocodile conservation breeding sanctuary in Zapata Swamp, Cuba.
Photo © Robin Moore, Re:wild

SAN QUINTIN KANGAROO RAT

Animal: San Quintin Kangaroo Rat
Class: Rodentia (Rodent)
Species: *Dipodomys gravipes*
Status: Critically Endangered
Population Trend: Unknown

It was a regular day in Baja California when a wildlife research team was just surveying a wildlife habitat and they discovered something small with a long tail. It was a different size than other kangaroo rats in the area. After taking measurements and comparing them to other species of kangaroo rats, they realized they had (accidentally!) rediscovered the lost San Quintin Kangaroo Rat, a species that hadn't been seen in over thirty years!

The largest member of the kangaroo rat fam, the San Quintin Kangaroo Rat is known for its much longer tail, accented nicely with a little tuft on the end. Another trademark of this kangaroo rat—or kangarat, if you will—is its impressive leaping ability. It can launch itself up to 3 feet (1 meter) in the air to escape (or at least surprise) its predators!

It's a Lifestyle

Burrowing is not only a hobby for the kangarat; it's a lifestyle. While it burrows to make its home, the San Quintin Kangaroo Rat also builds separate "pantries" where it stores the seeds it collects. By doing this, the species serves as an essential seed dispersal agent, spreading and "planting" seeds all over its range.

Aggressive Agriculture

To the surprise of many, predators like foxes and coyotes aren't actually driving this kangaroo rat to extinction. Instead, it's the result of the town of San Quintin in Mexico's Baja California becoming an agriculture hub. The area is being converted to fields and hothouses for strawberries and tomatoes—which are then exported to the United States at the expense of the San Quintin Kangaroo Rat's native habitat.

San Quintin Kangaroo Rat, Baja California, Mexico. Photo © Jonathan Alonso Villarreal Fletes, Terra Peninsular

Now that the San Quintin Kangaroo Rat has been rediscovered, researchers are hankering to learn more about the species, and conservationists are working to preserve their habitat. Conservationists are also trying to find other potential habitats for the kangaroo rat within the region. And everyone is looking for new strategies to protect the adorable rat and its ecosystem!

underfrog ● fact ●

The San Quintin Kangaroo Rat was formerly listed as Extinct by the Mexican government in 1994.

BAHAMA WARBLER

Animal: Bahama Warbler
Class: Aves (Bird)
Species: *Setophaga flavescens*
Status: Near Threatened
Population Trend: Decreasing

Would you ever look underneath a piece of tree bark on the forest floor for some tasty bugs to eat? No? Well, then, you must not be a Bahama Warbler! This small black and yellow bird is endemic to the pinewood habitat of Grand Bahama and Abaco Islands, and is known for "creeping" up and down the trunks of pine trees in search of its next meal.

The Damage of Dorian

Up until recently, this warbler's main threats were large-scale logging and forest fragmentation from roads and residential developments. And then in 2019, Hurricane Dorian ripped through the northwestern Bahamas. The Category 5 storm was the strongest hurricane to ever pass through The Bahamas and the worst recorded natural disaster in Bahamian history. Hurricane Dorian tore the island's landscape apart, leaving thousands of acres of warbler habitat completely destroyed in its wake.

When the storm finally ended, all relief efforts immediately—and rightfully—went to human rescues, relocations, and providing food and shelter for the people who were affected. But as time went on, people turned to focus on just how severe Dorian's environmental impact was. Forests, mangroves, coral reefs, and all of their ecosystems were ravaged.

Making "Point Counts" Count

Five months post-hurricane, Re:wild started working with the Bahamas National Trust (BNT), the National Geographic Foundation, the American Bird Conservancy, the National Audubon Society, and the Moore Charitable Foundation to assess just how much damage had been done to this bird species and its home. The majority of the ten-day trip was just conducting what we call "point counts" of birds, which literally just means counting how many of them we see. Thankfully, the bird had not vanished entirely, as we had feared.

While out in the wild, we also took stock of how many pine trees had been destroyed—which is obviously not the best news for our pine-dependent bird friend. It was clear that restoring pine forests had to be bumped up pretty high on our to-do list. As for what's next, we are working with BNT to launch a community conservation project to keep on monitoring the Bahama Warbler and its habitat.

underfrog ● fact ●

The Bahama Warbler is constantly confused with its doppelgänger, the Yellow-Throated Warbler. The main difference is that the Bahama Warbler has a *slightly* longer bill.

Bahama Warbler, northern Bahama islands.
Photo © Scott Johnson

UNION ISLAND GECKO

Animal: Union Island Gecko, aka Grenadines Clawed Gecko

Class: Reptilia (Reptile)

Species: *Gonatodes daudini*

Status: Critically Endangered

Population Trend: Stable

The Union Island Gecko is the cool bedazzled cousin of your everyday gecko. Also called the Grenadines Clawed Gecko, it has big red and black bull's-eye-looking marks on its back that have little spots of white in the middle. This almost makes it look like it has eyes going down its back. Although these little guys are only around 2.5 inches (6.35 centimeters) from snout to tail, they are still one of the most eye-catching animals in the Caribbean. The Union Island Gecko is named after its home of Union Island,
a quaint little spot in Saint Vincent and the Grenadines, where it can be found on just about any postcard or T-shirt in the local gift shops!

So Pretty It Hurts

In the case of threats, this gecko's showy looks have actually gotten it into trouble. Since it's *so* beautiful, it's become unfortunately popular in the pet trade, especially in Germany, the Netherlands, and Austria. It's so in demand that between 2010 and 2018, the Union Island Gecko's population dropped by around 80 percent. Today, it's estimated that no more than ten thousand Union Island Geckos still exist on the island.

Mobilizing the World to Save Geckos

How do we save this species? The government of Saint Vincent and the Grenadines have taken the lead by working with groups like Fauna & Flora International to set up remote poaching surveillance equipment, like camera traps. They're also overseeing the local community wardens in and around the habitat. Also helping out are all the countries that have signed on to the Convention on International Trade in Endangered Species of Wild Fauna and Flora, also known as CITES. They have voted to ban international trade of the Union Island Gecko. The ban grants officials all over the world the right to confiscate any geckos they find on the market. With all these conservation efforts, hopefully the Union Island Gecko will get to live on in more ways than just featuring on Caribbean postcards and tourists' T-shirts.

underfrog ● fact ●

The Union Island Gecko was only scientifically discovered in 2005.

Union Island Gecko, Union Island, Saint Vincent and the Grenadines.
Photo © Matthijs Kuijpers

VAQUITA

Animal: Vaquita
Class: Mammalia (Mammal)
Species: *Phocoena sinus*
Status: Critically Endangered
Population Trend: Decreasing

Let's talk about the "little cow" of the sea—the adorable pint-sized Vaquita! At 4.5 feet (1.37 meters) long, the Vaquita is the world's smallest cetacean (the family of whales, dolphins, and porpoises). Scientists and fisherpeople are not sure how the cute moniker originated, but it stuck. These "little cows" only exist right off the coast of Mexico in the northernmost part of the Gulf of California and are known to travel in groups of two to ten individuals. They eat mainly fish and some squids, and just bob around looking generally adorable.

The Remaining Ten

The Vaquita unfortunately holds the title of "most threatened marine mammal." While no one *really* knows for sure, researchers estimate that there are fewer than nineteen Vaquitas left on Earth, but there are probably more likely around ten. This is because the Vaquita is often a bycatch victim in gillnets for shrimp and finfish, which are now illegal in an established vaquita sanctuary in the Upper Gulf of California.

In the same part of the Gulf of California where the Vaquita lives, there's also a big fish called the Totoaba. The gillnets used to fish for Totoaba have a similar net mesh size to the Vaquita's head. Poachers use these illegal gillnets to catch Totoabas, but Vaquitas can easily get trapped in them too, and drown.

Giving Our Lives Porpoise

To save these little sea cows, our other partner, Sea Shepherd Conservation Society, is working with the Mexican government to stop the use and deployment of all gillnets that can catch Vaquita within the Vaquita Sanctuary. We also partnered with the National Marine Mammal Foundation to start the first Vaquita breeding program, called VaquitaCPR. The goal was to catch Vaquitas and protect them in a safe haven away from gillnets, but on one rescue mission, a female Vaquita died from stress. This loss halted the whole project, and now VaquitaCPR is focusing primarily on preventing the use of gillnets and supporting acoustic monitoring and community efforts.

During a field effort in 2018, Vaquita mother and calf pairs were spotted, and again the following year. Researchers in 2019 observed a group of mature Vaquitas swimming around with three new calves. If fishing with gillnets can be stopped, things could be looking up for this petite porpoise after all!

underfrog ●
fact ●

The word *vaquita* actually translates to "little cow" in Spanish.

Vaquita, Sea of Cortez, Mexico.
Photo © Jonas Teilmann, VaquitaCPR

SPINY GIANT FROG

Animal: Spiny Giant Frog
Class: Amphibia (Amphibian)
Species: *Eleutherodactylus nortoni*
Status: Critically Endangered
Population Trend: Decreasing

The Spiny Giant Frog, or Norton's Robber Frog, is super rare and is found only in the mountains of southwestern Haiti and the Dominican Republic. Like many frog species, the Spiny Giant Frog uses its call to identify members of its own species. In one sequence, the Spiny Giant Frog slides between five notes and ends on a whistle tone—in the stylings of the iconic Mariah Carey, of course—making them strong contenders for a record deal.

Wanted: Protection for Protected Areas

Scientists anticipate that the Spiny Giant Frog may have an 80 percent population decline within the next ten years because of habitat destruction. Most of this habitat destruction is caused by agriculture and also wood extraction for charcoal production. In Haiti, the Tiburon Peninsula and Massif de la Selle are being farmed left and right, and the same thing is happening in the frogs' only known habitat in the Dominican Republic. The Spiny Giant Frog also lives in five national parks in Haiti: Macaya, Morne La Viste, Grand Bois, Deux Mamelles, and Grande Colline. Despite their status as protected areas, habitat destruction is still an issue, and the Spiny Giant Frog's home continues to be destroyed.

"Reserved" for Someone Special

Looking for a way to help, Re:wild got together with several partners in 2019 to establish the first-*ever* private nature reserve in Haiti! It consists of over 1,200 acres (almost 5 square kilometers) on Grand Bois Mountain. Over sixty-eight vertebrate species live there, including many teetering on the brink of extinction. It's also home to the largest number of frog species in the Caribbean! The reserve has been recognized as a Key Biodiversity Area, a place that is critical for the global persistence of biodiversity and overall health of the planet. With this new protected area, Spiny Giant Frogs should see their numbers on the up-and-up. But still, improved management of other protected areas is going to be critical for these big froggos going forward.

underfrog ●
fact ●

This web-toed popstar-in-the-making lives in sinkhole caves and sometimes even under the tree cover at coffee bean farms.

Spiny Giant Frog, Haiti. Photo © Robin Moore, Re:wild

HELLBENDER

Animal: Hellbender
Class: Amphibia (Amphibian)
Species: *Cryptobranchus alleganiensis*
Status: Near Threatened
Population Trend: Decreasing

Known by not one but two iconic names, the Hellbender is also called the "snot otter" because of the light layer of slime coating its slithery bod. Not to mention the plethora of monikers given to it by locals: "mud devil," "devil dog," "ground puppy," "Allegheny alligator," and, of course, our personal favorite, "lasagna lizard." (Though they are not lizards or alligators, obviously not puppies, and certainly not devils or a noodley dish!)

Measuring in at around an impressive 2.5 feet (0.76 meters), the Hellbender is officially America's largest salamander and the third-largest salamander in the world. It lives a rather secret, off-the-grid life under rocks in streams and rivers all the way from southern New York to the northern parts of Alabama and Georgia, and as far west as Illinois. In New York, the "snot otter" can only be found in the Susquehanna and Allegheny Rivers and their tributaries.

The Amazing "Breathing Wrinkles"

Something oddly cool about the Hellbender is that it has lungs! (Full disclosure: They're largely nonfunctional.) Instead, this "lasagna lizard" mostly breathes through skin flaps on its sides, which absorb oxygen from cold water. As awesome as these "breathing wrinkles" are, they also make the Hellbender *super* sensitive to water pollution. Agriculture near their home causes dirt, fertilizers, and other muck to get dumped into local streams, messing with their water quality. And while it's not that big of a deal *yet*, researchers are keeping an eye on a fungal pathogen called Bsal that they think could wreak havoc on the salamander if the pathogen spreads to North America.

The Children (Baby Hellbenders) Are the Future

Hellbenders have gotten a bit of a head start thanks to researchers in New York State who've started hatching and raising baby Hellbenders in human care. Once the babies grow to around 9 inches (23 centimeters) long, they are released back into the Allegheny River. Entering the wild at this size increases the babies' chances of

Male Hellbenders fight over mating territory, Southern Appalachia, United States. Photo © David Herasimtschuks, *Freshwaters Illustrated*

survival. What's more, several zoos even offered to take in some Hellbender babies and raise their own colonies. Get ready to practice your citizen science skills; we'll all have to keep a lookout for the "lasagna lizard" together!

underfrog ● fact ●

The slimy mucus that coats the Hellbender's body is presumed to protect them from abrasion and parasites.

PADDLEFISH

Animal: Paddlefish, aka Spoonbill Catfish
Class: Actinopterygii (Fish)
Species: *Polyodon spathula*
Status: Vulnerable
Population Trend: Unknown

Up to 8 FEET (2.43 METERS) LONG. 150-PLUS POUNDS (68 KILOGRAMS). PREHISTORIC. The Paddlefish is basically your Jurassic Park dream—it's a fish older than the dinosaurs that not even a meteor could stop. Today, this freshwater fish usually lives in big, deep rivers with slow currents. They're unmistakable with their long, flat snouts called rostrums. These rostrums are actually covered with electroreceptors that help the Paddlefish, aka the Spoonbill Cat, better understand its environment. Through changing electrical fields, the rostrums can locate microscopic animal prey (zooplankton) and even help the Paddlefish navigate its migration route. More interestingly, they look kind of funny. But in an *endearing* way, we swear!

This dinosaur-adjacent species is also known for swimming with its mouth open, which, in all honesty, doesn't really help with the whole not-being-funny-looking thing. It just looks like it's perpetually frowning. But here's the kicker— when it's doing this, the Paddlefish is actually filter feeding and ventilating its gills at the same time! A natural multitasker!

Too *Dam* Bad

In the past, the Paddlefish has been hunted for its meat and its eggs, which have been sold as expensive caviar. These days, its biggest threats are habitat destruction and modification—caused by dams all over the Mississippi River basin. Dam construction blocked access to the Paddlefish's usual spawning sites and split up their populations, generally putting a *dam*-per on their reproduction.

Restockin' the Rivers

In 1991, a whole organization was founded to establish new rules and regulations about fishing in the Mississippi River basin. It's called the Mississippi Interstate Cooperative Resource Association, or MICRA, and their first order of business was to restock the rivers with Paddlefish over the next five years. And since 1994, over a million hatchery-reared babies have been tagged and released into the wild! Thanks to said tagging and releasing, there are now more than ten thousand adult Paddlefish out there. Sounds like things are going pretty *dam* well!

underfrog ●
fact ●

The Paddlefish's genus name, *Polyodon*, is Greek for "many tooth"—a reference to their hundreds and hundreds of gill rakers that filter water and help the Paddlefish feed.

Paddlefish, Gavins Point National Fish Hatchery, South Dakota, United States. Photo © Ryan Hagerty, USFWS

MARIANA FRUIT BAT

Animal: Mariana Fruit Bat, aka Fanihi
Class: Mammalia (Mammal)
Species: *Pteropus mariannus*
Status: Endangered
Population Trend: Decreasing

The Mariana Fruit Bat belongs to the genus *Pteropus*, which is pronounced "terror-pus" since the *P* is silent. All bats from this genus are called "flying foxes" because of their big eyes and adorable puppy-like faces. So, you know this species is pretty freakin' cute! These "flying foxes" are only one of two mammals that are native to the island of Guam and the Commonwealth of the Northern Mariana Islands (CNMI).

Mariana Fruit Bats can be found in the native limestone forests and along the coasts where they feed on fruit and nectar. During the day, they roost in trees in groups that range from small to colonies of over a thousand on the island of Rota. These colonies are often located in hard-to-reach places, like the sides of cliffs, where they can, for the most part, get some peace and quiet.

A Devastating Delicacy

The Mariana Fruit Bat has been important to the Chamorros—the Indigenous people of the Mariana Islands—for thousands of years. In the Chamorro culture, the Mariana Fruit Bat's meat is considered a delicacy. Before World War I, hunting was done with tools like spears and slings. However, after World War I, firearms became freely available, allowing hunting at a longer range and with less skill. It resulted in many more bats being killed each year—too many at a time. By the 1970s, they were declared Endangered on Guam and, soon afterward, in the CNMI.

A Plummeting Population

Illegal hunting is still a serious threat to the bats on all the Mariana Islands, but on Guam the biggest threat is the invasive Brown Tree Snake—which eats the bats' babies.

Habitat destruction from human development also affects the bats, but typhoons cause the biggest drop in numbers when they pass near or over the islands. For instance, between three thousand and four thousand bats lived in Rota in 2015. When a typhoon passed through that year, their numbers were cut in half. And just when the Mariana Fruit Bat's population started to grow again, another typhoon hit Rota in 2018 and set them back once again.

What's Next?

Guam's Division of Aquatic and Wildlife Resources (DAWR) and the local people are working to increase the numbers of the Mariana Fruit Bat. People can help the bats by planting fruit trees in their own yards! And if they see bats visiting the trees, they can contact DAWR and tell them about it.

underfrog ●
fact ●

While their life span in the wild is unknown, the Mariana Fruit Bat can live up to thirty years under human care.

Mariana Fruit Bat, Island of Guam, unincorporated territory of the United States.
Photo © MerlinTuttle.org, Science Source

RINGTAIL

Animal: Ringtail
Class: Mammalia (Mammal)
Species: *Bassariscus astutus*
Status: Least Concern
Population Trend: Unknown

Ah, yes—the Ringtail! This cat-sized carnivore's trademark is its big fluffy tail with fourteen to sixteen rings. It has giant marble eyes and upright ears that fully equip it for nocturnal living, making it a skilled nighttime hunter and forager. It lives all over Mexico and in the western and southwestern United States and can adapt to live in an industrial setting if it needs to. One of the coolest things about the Ringtail is that it basically hasn't changed at all for twenty-five million years! Because of this, people often refer to it as a living fossil. So, yes—they've always been this cute!

The Ringtail goes by many different names, all of which speak to its personality. When you break down its scientific name, *Bassariscus astutus*, *bassar* means "fox," *isc* means "little," and *astut* means "cunning," so you get "cunning little fox." In Mexico, ringtails are often called *cacomistles*, which is Spanish for "nimble thieves." Early American settlers even kept these very historically mischievous Ringtails in their homes as both companions and mousers. This earned them yet *another* nickname: the "miner's cat"!

Getting Pelted

The fur trade is easily the biggest threat to the Ringtail, which can be legally hunted in a few states. In recent years alone, about five thousand Ringtails have been captured annually for pelts in two states. Sadly, it's also pretty common for Ringtails to get caught in traps intended for foxes and raccoons. They are also too often hit by cars when they try to cross the road.

Least Concern, Most Cunning

As for Ringtail conservation efforts, not much is being done right now. But then again, this "cunning little fox" is so far listed as Least Concern. Conservationists will jump to action if needed, but for now, let's hope it stays this way.

underfrog fact

The Ringtail's ankle joints can rotate up to 180 degrees, making them impressively agile climbers!

Ringtail, Chiricahua Mountains, Arizona, United States. Photo © Bruce D. Taubert

HAWAIIAN TREE SNAIL

Animal: Hawaiian Tree Snail
Class: Gastropoda (Gastropod)
Species: *Partulina mighelsiana*
Status: Endangered
Population Trend: Unspecified

Have you ever heard of George the Hawaiian Tree Snail? He was the last known member of his species. Researchers searched high and low for another of George's species for him to mate with, but they had no luck, making George the world's loneliest snail. Though "Lonely George" sadly never graduated to "Lucky George," his life remained full of beauty and purpose: He served as the face of Hawaiian snail conservation!

Long ago, there were 750 different snail species on the Hawaiian Islands; now there are about 200 species, many of which are tree snails. Snails on the islands of Oahu and Molokai are known for their diverse and richly colored candy-striped shells. They're also famous in Hawaiian folklore. Legend has it that they "sing" as they move up and down trees. Native Hawaiian people have even gone as far as calling them "the voice of the forest."

Funky and "Gunky"

Hawaiian Tree Snails are also some frequently overlooked ecological power players. They have even been hailed as "gunk specialists"! When they eat said "gunk"—meaning all the fungi that grows on leaves—they're actually eating all the excess fungi and, in doing so, maintaining the overall fungal diversity. This may even protect the host trees from disease. It would be a win-win-win, fungi-wise!

Not So "Rosy"

Let's put it this way: Certain invasive species haven't done the Hawaiian Tree Snail any favors. The Rosy Wolfsnail is a big problem for them. Native to the southeastern United States, the Rosy Wolfsnail was originally brought to Hawaii to eat other invasive mollusks like the Giant African Snail. The Rosy Wolfsnail seemed to think the Hawaiian Tree Snail tasted a heck of a lot better than the Giant African Snail, and has been eating them to near-extinction since its debut in 1955.

Hawaiian Tree Snail, island of Molokai, Hawaii, United States. Photo © David Sischo, Hawaii Department of Land and Natural Resources

New Discovery (S)Nails It

To save the snails, scientists with the Hawaii Invertebrate Program and the Snail Extinction Prevention Program (SEPP) have been working to protect remaining snails and also trying to build new populations. In 2020, they received some good news when a scientist discovered a new species of snail: *Auriculella gagneorum*. Finding this new snail proved that maybe there is still hope for Hawaiian Tree Snails, which would be a great tribute to George!

underfrog ●
fact ●

All tree snails are hermaphrodites, but a snail still needs to find another snail to reproduce.

LOST SPECIES:
DWARF HUTIA

Animal: Dwarf Hutia

Class: Mammalia (Mammal)

Species: *Mesocapromys nanus*

Status: Critically Endangered

Population Trend: Unknown

Last Seen: 1937

One of the first mammals to be described just from a fossil alone, the Dwarf Hutia is kind of a guinea pig–esque rodent that once lived all over Cuba and the nearby Isle of Youth. It was last captured by researchers in 1937, but some suspicious poops found in 1978 might have been enough to prove that it's still out there! If it does still exist, the Dwarf Hutia would most likely be living in the uber-remote Zapata Swamp, and there would only be a handful of them left.

So, what wiped these little guys out? Invasive species came in hot; there was some competition with Black Rats and predation by mongooses and the invasive Clarias Catfish, one of the most vicious predators in the Zapata Swamp. On top of that, there was general human-caused habitat destruction, and a couple accidental fires in Zapata Swamp. If we have any chance of uncovering the Dwarf Hutia, we need to better survey Zapata Swamp and manage its invasive species.

underfrog ● fact ●

Unlike many other rodents—who usually have many offspring in a litter—a Dwarf Hutia that was captured back in the day only gave birth to one baby.

BLANCO BLIND SALAMANDER

Animal: Blanco Blind Salamander

Class: Amphibia (Amphibian)

Species: *Eurycea robusta*

Status: Data Deficient

Population Trend: Unknown

Last Seen: 1951

The Blanco Blind Salamander is *so rare* that it has quite literally only been found once—in a spot slightly northeast of San Marcos, Texas. It was discovered back in 1951 by workers excavating a small crevice with flowing water in the bed of the then-dry Blanco River. Over the years, the river has changed course, and the spring is now buried under gravel and sediment. Unfortunately, we do not know if this salamander is still there.

If any species were going to survive being plugged back into a river orifice, it would probably be the Blanco Blind Salamander. Unsurprisingly, it's blind. It breathes through gills, is colorless, and is suspected to eat groundwater invertebrates and even other salamanders in the aquifers where it lives. Possibly the greatest threat to this species is declining quantity and quality of water in the small portion of the Edwards Aquifer that it calls home. Its only threat is considered to be aquifer degradation (underwater rocks getting ruined), but again, no one *really* knows for sure.

underfrog ● fact ●

Only four Blanco Blind Salamanders were found at the time of their scientific discovery.

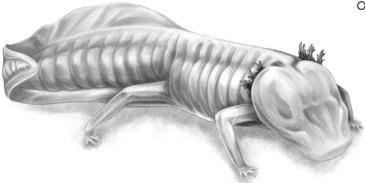

JACQUELINE LITZGUS

Name: Dr. Jacqueline Litzgus
Spotted Turtle Expert
Specialty: Spotted Turtles
Title: Professor, Department of Biology, Science, Engineering and Architecture
Organization: Laurentian University

Dr. Jacqueline Litzgus is basically the unofficial champion of the Spotted Turtle. A biologist and professor at Laurentian University in Ontario, Canada, Dr. Litzgus can often be found in waders, trudging through wetlands, and teaching students how to stand up for the little guy. (The "little guy" being Spotted Turtles, in this case.)

Dr. Litzgus has spent her professional career (thirty years!) focusing on the ecological factors that make Spotted Turtles the way that they are. She's published a bunch of research papers on everything from their seasonal activity and how they hibernate, to how long they live, to their home ranges. Dr. Litzgus is also quite the turtle advocate—apparently, turtle poachers sometimes turn to academic papers for clues about where to find the species. Because of this, Dr. Litzgus makes sure she never reveals the location of the Spotted Turtles she studies. If she did tell us, she says, she'd "have to kill us"—like a spy protecting super secret and important information.

Dr. Jacqueline Litzgus, Ontario, Canada.
Photo © James Baxter-Gilbert

Perhaps her biggest accomplishment to date is popularizing the phrase "butt breathing" in her academic writing. Overall, Dr. Jacqueline Litzgus is a total legend, both in the world of turtles and in ours.

SCOTT JOHNSON

Name: Scott Johnson
Bahamian Bird and Reptile Expert
Specialty: The Bahamas, Birds, and Reptiles
Title: Biologist, Science Officer
Organization: Bahamas National Trust

Scott Johnson, a biologist and science officer with the Bahamas National Trust, is known for his infectious love of birds and reptiles and his masterful snake-charming skills! Scott first got his start in animal conservation while attending the College of the Bahamas (COB), where he studied biology and chemistry and moonlit as a lab technician.

It was in college that Scott worked as a research assistant with the Kirtland's Warbler Research and Training Project and learned all about birds, their ecosystems, and how to translate all of that into data. He was so successful as a research assistant that he was awarded a scholarship to St. Mary's College of Maryland to finish undergrad!

These days, Scott spends his time going on field research expeditions to study seabirds, iguanas, flamingoes, and snakes—just to drop a couple names—and helping educate other Bahamians on the importance of their local species. Scott also plans to pursue his doctorate in biology, with a focus on the birds and reptiles of The Bahamas. We don't have any doubts that Scott will accomplish this and much more!

BNT Science Officer Scott Johnson holding a Bahamian Racer, Andros Island, The Bahamas.
Photo © David B. Jones, Clamflats Photos

South and Central America

STARRY NIGHT HARLEQUIN TOAD

Animal: Starry Night Harlequin Toad
Class: Amphibia (Amphibian)
Species: *Atelopus arsyecue*
Status: Critically Endangered
Population Trend: Decreasing

After scientists feared the Starry Night Harlequin Toad was Extinct for over thirty years, the toad officially emerged from the ominous cloak of darkness! Named for its shiny black skin with white speckles and the clear, dark skies in its mountain habitat of Colombia, the Starry Night Harlequin Toad looks just like a fallen piece of night sky.

This toad can only be found in Sierra Nevada de Santa Marta, aka one of the tallest—and most remote—mountain ranges on Earth. The toads share this area with the Indigenous Arhuaco community of Sogrome, who know them as "gouna." The Arhuaco people consider the Starry Night Harlequin Toad sacred and have invited scientists to research and help manage the special speckled species.

SAVE THE GENUS!

Unfortunately, Starry Night Harlequin Toads and their entire genus are the most threatened group of amphibians in the whole world. Harlequin toads have been hit hard by chytridiomycosis, a disease caused by a fungus called chytrid.

Out of all ninety-six known species of harlequin toads, eighty are considered Endangered, Critically Endangered, or Extinct in the wild. If we don't do something drastic, scientists fear harlequin toads could be the latest genus of vertebrates to go extinct in the wild in modern history.

Mixing the Ancestral with the Scientific

What are people doing to help? Well, Re:wild is a leading partner in the Atelopus Survival Initiative, an initiative that is bringing together harlequin toad experts around the world to coordinate an emergency response to the crisis. As part of the ASI, Re:wild partners with Fundación Atelopus, which sent researchers to work with the Arhuaco people on expeditions into Sierra Nevada de Santa Marta in search of the Starry

Starry Night Harlequin Toad, Sogrome, Sierra Nevada de Santa Marta, Colombia. Photo © José Luis Pérez González, Fundación Atelopus

Night Harlequin Toad. Researchers stayed in the Arhuaco people's homes, learned their cultural philosophies, and spent time getting to know them. Together, they then combined their ancestral and scientific knowledge to come up with a conservation plan that both can get behind. Teamwork makes the toad dream work!

underfrog fact

Even though the Starry Night Harlequin Toad has been lost to science for nearly thirty years, it has never been lost to members of the Sogrome community, who have always lived in harmony with the toad. The toad acts as an indicator to the community about when to plant crops or perform spiritual ceremonies.

JACKSON'S CLIMBING SALAMANDER

Animal: Jackson's Climbing Salamander, aka Jackson's Mushroomtongue Salamander
Class: Amphibia (Amphibian)
Species: *Bolitoglossa jacksoni*
Status: Critically Endangered
Population Trend: Decreasing

Behold, the "Golden Wonder"! More formally known as Jackson's Climbing Salamander, this little amphibian is recognizable by its vibrant honey yellow color and the lone black stripe down its back. It seems hard to miss, yet somehow this reclusive species managed to stay out of the public eye for *forty-two years*!

The first of our 25 Most Wanted Lost Species to be rediscovered, the Jackson's Climbing Salamander was found in 2017 when a park guard took a lunch break during his usual rounds at Guatemala's Finca San Isidro Amphibian Reserve. Since its scientific discovery in the mid-1970s, the park guard was only the third person to report setting eyes on this salamander in over four decades!

Tough Terrain

The Jackson's Climbing Salamander lives in the Cuchumatanes mountain range, which—take it from us—is some pretty tough terrain. It gets cold and wet and super steep and is exhausting to trudge through, but the Jackson's Climbing Salamander manages just fine even though it's only 2.5 inches (6.35 centimeters) long. But add in some climate change, and you've got severe weather, which makes it hard to survive. Climate change—along with deforestation—is likely taking its toll on this species.

A Home for Lost Salamanders

Re:wild has helped establish—and expand—the Finca San Isidro Amphibian Reserve (officially the Yal Unin Yul Witz Reserve) for Guatemala's local frog and salamander populations. We did it just in the nick of time, before the land could be turned into a coffee plantation. The forests are also home to two other once-lost salamander species: the Finca Chiblac Salamander and the Long-Limbed Salamander. Everyone involved in establishing the reserve hoped we'd rediscover Jackson's Climbing Salamander there again, and, amazingly, we did! Hopefully, this suction-legged "Golden Wonder" will be the first of many, many more of our lost species to be found.

underfrog ●
fact ●

The Jackson's Climbing Salamander scales trees using little suckers on its legs.

Jackson's Climbing Salamander, Yal Unin Yul Witz Reserve, Guatemala.
Photo © Carlos Vásquez, FUNDAECO

TITICACA WATER FROG

Animal: Titicaca Water Frog
Class: Amphibia (Amphibian)
Species: *Telmatobius culeus*
Status: Endangered
Population Trend: Decreasing

With a body that measures about 8 inches (20 centimeters) in length, the Titicaca Water Frog clocks in as one of the largest of the known species of water frog. This slimy loaf is completely aquatic, making its home in its beloved namesake in Bolivia and Peru's Lake Titicaca. The frog can also be found in the surrounding lagoons that flow into the lake and some nearby ponds, although it does prefer to hang out at the bottom of the lake most of the time.

Sidebar about Water Frogs

All sixty-three known species of water frogs are originally from the Andean highlands in South America and don't tend to travel too far. While the Titicaca Water Frog is entirely aquatic, some water frogs are semiaquatic, meaning they go between chilling on land and in the water.

When they do decide to go for a dip, water frogs generally prefer frigid temperatures. They like it so cold that researchers who go out in the field to study them find that their hands go completely numb.

The Curse of the "Green Smoothie"

The Titicaca Water Frog is—*uh*, how do we put this lightly?—in trouble as the result of an onslaught of threats. They have to deal with water pollution in Lake Titicaca, disease caused by the chytrid fungus, and dishes with frog legs and "green smoothies." In certain parts of Peru, people make these so-called green smoothies by blending these frogs into a juice—they believe it can cure just about anything from asthma to osteoporosis.

(continued) ▶

Titicaca Water Frog, Isla de la Luna, Lake Titicaca, Bolivia.
Photo © Arturo Muñoz

Stopping the Sewage

Multiple times between 2009 and 2020, there were massive die-offs of the Titicaca Water Frog. Researchers believe this has something to do with increased sewage runoff and runoff from mining. Because of this, conservationists brought a bunch of scientific experts, local community members, park rangers, and government officials together to figure out how to prevent more pollution and raise awareness for the Titicaca Water Frog. In more recent years, the Bolivian and Peruvian governments have also stepped up by signing an agreement outlining plans to reduce pollutants through wastewater treatment and solid waste management. With all these steps in place, there is still hope for the Titicaca Water Frog and all of its other froggy friends.

underfrog ● fact ●

Even though the Titicaca Water Frog has lungs, it mostly breathes through the folds in its skin, absorbing oxygen from water.

NORTHERN MURIQUI MONKEY

Animal: Northern Muriqui Monkey
Class: Mammalia (Mammal)
Species: *Brachyteles hypoxanthus*
Status: Critically Endangered
Population Trend: Decreasing

Called the "hippie primate" because of their chilled-out, peaceful lifestyle, the Northern Muriqui Monkey is just about the best possible role model for humans. Instead of fighting, these monkeys just hang out in trees and hug each other!

Despite being so happy-go-lucky, the Northern Muriqui Monkey is sadly one of the most Critically Endangered primates on Earth. At this point, fewer than one thousand individuals are left out there, all living in a dozen *very* fragmented parts of Brazil's Atlantic Forest.

Lack of Exposure and Too Much of Everything Else

Habitat destruction and hunting have put a big dent in the numbers of Northern Muriqui Monkeys left in the wild. Agriculture is growing in Brazil, and much of the forest has been destroyed because of it. Experts also blame some of the muriqui's decline on its lack of exposure, meaning the majority of Brazilians don't even know it exists! Take all this and add in cattle ranching and urbanization, and you've got a recipe for disaster.

(continued) ▶

Restoring Peace to the Hippie Monkey

One of Re:wild's fantastic senior associate conservation scientists, Dr. Karen Strier, is more or less single-handedly responsible for reviving this muriqui species. Since 1983, Dr. Strier has been the director of the Muriqui Project of Caratinga, a program that works with students and partners from Brazil and all over the world in one of the last remaining strongholds for the Northern Muriqui Monkey. This place is a privately owned and federally protected reserve called the RPPN Feliciano Miguel Abdala. There, Dr. Strier and her students focus on the muriqui's behavioral ecology, reproductive biology, life history, and—of course—how to save them and their habitat!

Thanks to their work, the population of Northern Muriqui Monkeys in the reserve is up from 50 in 1983 to about 250 today! Based on what they've done so far, we know that Dr. Strier and her team are on the right track to restore peace and bring good juju to the hippie monkey once again!

underfrog ● fact ●

The Northern Muriqui Monkey was pitched as the official mascot for the Rio 2016 Olympics, but unfortunately it didn't make the cut.

Northern Muriqui Monkey at the RPPN Feliciano Miguel Abdala reserve, Minas Gerais, Brazil.
Photo © Carla B. Possamai, Projeto Muriqui de Caratinga

GOLDEN LION TAMARIN

Animal: Golden Lion Tamarin

Class: Mammalia (Mammal)

Species: *Leontopithecus rosalia*

Status: Endangered

Population Trend: Decreasing

The best stories are conservation success stories, and Golden Lion Tamarins have quite the story. Golden Lion Tamarins are known for their reddish-goldish manes and for being a heck of a lot smaller than most other monkeys. Golden Lion Tamarins usually weigh around 1.3 pounds (0.6 kilograms) and measure about 25 inches (63.5 centimeters) from the tip of their nose to the tip of their tail, but the majority of those inches come from their *long* tail. The Golden Lion Tamarin can only be found in the lowland area of Brazil's Atlantic Forest right by the city of Rio de Janeiro. There, only 2 percent of the small monkey's original habitat remains.

Fragmented from Friends

For this little monkey, habitat destruction is easily its biggest threat—there are roadways built every day as a result of urbanization in Brazil. This road construction also means the Golden Lion Tamarin's population has been fragmented into smaller groups, living in pockets of rainforest separated by development. These newly divided, smaller subpopulations are believed to have reached carrying capacity, meaning the small forest islands can't sustain more of them. Golden Lion Tamarins are also captured for the pet trade and have recently had to deal with a gnarly yellow fever outbreak too.

(continued) ▶

Golden Lion Tamarin, Fazenda Apetiba, Rio de Janeiro State, Brazil.
Photo © Russ Mittermeier, Re:wild

Golden Conservation

The Golden Lion Tamarin has been considered a poster child for conservation success in Brazil—and the world—for over half a century. After being brought back from the brink of extinction by a conservation breeding program, which released tamarins born in zoos to the wild, everyone had hailed the Golden Lion Tamarin as a conservation success story—and then yellow fever struck. Researchers estimate that yellow fever killed off about 30 percent of the restored Golden Lion Tamarin population. Scientists quickly developed a vaccine to protect these monkeys from yellow fever, but once it was ready to administer, COVID-19 hit, and the process was delayed. Smaller teams were able to start vaccinating the monkeys in 2020 under strict social distancing protocols, with the goal of vaccinating at least five hundred Golden Lion Tamarins. This was the smallest number of vaccinations that would make it possible for these wild populations to continue to thrive.

underfrog ● fact ●

Brazil put the sweet face of the Golden Lion Tamarin on a banknote as a symbol of endangered species in Brazil.

MARINE IGUANA

Animal: Marine Iguana
Class: Reptilia (Reptile)
Species: *Amblyrhynchus cristatus*
Status: Vulnerable
Population Trend: Decreasing

When Charles Darwin described Marine Iguanas, he called them "hideous-looking" and the "most disgusting, clumsy lizards." No offense to Mr. Darwin, but beauty is in the eye of the beholder, and these iguanas are magnificent. Marine Iguanas are adapted to a life spent basking in the sun on the Galápagos Islands' rocky shores and foraging in the sea. They are the only lizards in the world that hang out *in* the ocean, where they swim with a grace that defies Darwin's unflattering description, their bodies and tails curving like ribbons through the water.

The Marine Iguana's origin story is still kind of an enigma. Most scientists believe that some type of South American land iguana must've floated out to sea on some driftwood and somehow wound up in the Galápagos. The land iguana spread throughout all the islands in the archipelago, and then evolved into a bunch of different iguana species. This is why each island's Marine Iguana has adapted to have its own shape, color, and quirks!

Today, these hefty reptiles have evolved to be gentle herbivores with strong crocodile-like tails and dark skin that absorbs sunlight to warm them up after taking a dip in the freezing Galápagos waters. They even have glands near their noses that expel salt.

Feral Rats, Cats, Dogs, and Climate Change—Oh My!

At 4–5 feet (1–1.5 meters) long, you'd think the Marine Iguana wouldn't have a lot to worry about predator-wise. However, non-native rats and feral cats and dogs found a loophole—instead of going after the big guys, they feed on

(continued) ▶

the iguana's eggs and young. Intense temperature changes have also messed with algae around the archipelagos, making the availability of the Marine Iguana's favorite food supply pretty inconsistent.

Population Protocol

The whole Marine Iguana population lives within three separate protected areas. Because the Galápagos is such a hot tourist destination, a lot of Ecuadorian mainlanders come to the islands in search of tourist industry jobs. To prevent the Galápagos from getting overpopulated—and subsequently running the iguanas off the land—Ecuador has required a special visa to visit the Galápagos, and there are strict requirements on who can move there.

underfrog ●
fact ●

The Marine Iguana sneezes out of their salt glands to get rid of the salt they ingest underwater during lunch time.

Marine Iguana, Galápagos Islands.
Photo © Cristina Mittermeier

LONG-TAILED CHINCHILLA

Animal: Long-Tailed Chinchilla
Class: Mammalia (Mammal)
Species: *Chinchilla lanigera*
Status: Endangered
Population Trend: Decreasing

Chinchillas: You know them and you love them, and who in their right mind wouldn't? They're living, breathing cotton balls! With such soft, thick fur and general adorableness, Long-Tailed Chinchillas are, unsurprisingly, popular pets.

These little floofballs can only be found in the wilds in Chile, where they live anywhere from the ocean side up to the arid mountain slopes of the western Andes.

Pummeled by Hunting

The Long-Tailed Chinchilla's biggest threat is the fur trade. With their pelts becoming more popular in the late 1800s, chinchillas were almost completely hunted to extinction. Long-Tailed Chinchilla populations struggle to recover from hunting in part because they reproduce really slowly. There aren't enough babies being born to make up for chinchillas lost. Besides this high-stakes hunting, chinchillas also have to deal with the ever-looming threats of grazing animals, deforestation, and harm from mining.

Protect the Wild Cotton Ball!

In 1983, the government of Chile set up Las Chinchillas National Reserve, which is listed today as a Key Biodiversity Area, making it critical to the health of the planet and the persistence of biodiversity. This reserve protects much of the world's Long-Tailed Chinchilla population. One of Re:wild's partners, Save the Wild Chinchillas, started conservation work on this species back in 1995, and all their efforts with researching, restoring habitat, and gaining community support have resulted in increases in the size of the chinchilla colonies directly outside of the protected areas. With more folks falling in love with them and pitching in to help, we'd say this long-tailed cotton ball species can look forward to some brighter days ahead.

underfrog ●
fact ●

While lots of chinchillas are bred commercially as pets,
Long-Tailed Chinchillas are considered Endangered because
there are so few of them still in the wild.

Long-Tailed Chinchilla, Smithsonian's National Zoo, United States. Photo © Connor Mallon, Smithsonian's National Zoo

CENTRAL AMERICAN RIVER TURTLE

Animal: Central American River Turtle, aka Hicatee

Class: Reptilia (Reptile)

Species: *Dermatemys mawii*

Status: Critically Endangered

Population Trend: Decreasing

The Central American River Turtle, also called the Hicatee, is the last remaining species from a long line of turtles—and when we say a long line, we mean a *long* line—like, *sixty-five million years* long.

The Hicatee lives in Central America, specifically Belize, southern Mexico, and northern Guatemala. It's herbivorous and completely aquatic, making itself cozy in deep rivers and lakes. During the wet season, it enjoys a little change of scenery and heads off to flooded forests to nest, only ever leaving the water to lay its eggs.

A Daunting Delicacy

While the Central American River Turtle's life sounds super mellow and unbothered, this reptile is sadly one of the most threatened freshwater turtles on the planet. This is mostly the result of overhunting throughout its range because its meat is considered a delicacy. It's caught in nets by free divers and by harpooning. While selling Hicatee meat has been illegal in Belize since 2003, this hasn't done enough to stop it from being harvested. If things keep going the way that they're going, the Central American River Turtle will likely be driven to extinction.

You Better Belize It!

In 2010, the Turtle Survival Alliance and the Belize Foundation for Research and Environmental Education (BFREE) held the first-ever Hicatee conservation forum in Belize. It was there that a bunch of scientists, government officials, and nonprofit organizations got together to share information about the Hicatee and come up with new ways to save it. The result was a conservation breeding program at BFREE in southern Belize where they breed animals by the hundreds every year! The program is expanding now that we know the species has a chance of survival. Looking forward, the protection laws currently in place will have to be enforced more strictly, and conservationists will have to work with communities to develop alternative opportunities for those who wish to harvest the Hicatee. It's the only way we can save one of the last quasi-dinosaurs out there.

underfrog ●
fact ●

The ancient family of turtles that the Hicatee belongs to is known as Dermatemyidae, a family that first showed up in Asia during the Cretaceous period before spreading to Europe, Africa, and North and Central America.

Central American River Turtle, photographed as part of the Belize Turtle Ecology Lab, Belize.
Photo © Donald McKnight

BAIRD'S TAPIR

Animal: Baird's Tapir
Class: Mammalia (Mammal)
Species: *Tapirus bairdii*
Status: Endangered
Population Trend: Decreasing

Roll a deer, a rhino, and an anteater together, and you'd probably get something that looks like the tapir. Known as the "gardeners of the forest," tapirs eat a whole bunch of plants, fruits, and seeds, and then disperse all the seeds through their poop. By spreading seeds of certain slow-growing trees—especially ones that trap and store carbon—tapirs are one of the key players in our fight against climate change! And in the future, these long-nosed animals, who are actually relatives of horses and rhinos, could be instrumental in helping countries live up to their climate change agreements!

Altogether, there are four species of tapir: Mountain Tapir, Malay Tapir, Lowland Tapir, and Baird's Tapir. Baird's Tapirs are the largest animals native to Central America. These guys have long noses that are more like short elephant trunks that help them grab branches and leaves that would otherwise be out of reach. The Baird's Tapir is the national animal of Belize, where it's lovingly known as "the mountain cow."

Tapir-ing Off

The biggest threats to Baird's Tapirs are habitat destruction and hunting. Between 2001 and 2010, Mexico and Central America lost about 70,000 square miles (181,000 square kilometers) of forest habitat due to expanding agriculture and climate change. As this was happening, the forests became fragmented, pushing populations of tapir further apart, both physically and genetically. More recently, cattle ranches have started causing some problems for the Baird's Tapir by wiping out more of its habitat and replacing it with—you guessed it—cattle pasture. The Baird's Tapir also reproduces very slowly, which means their numbers are going down a lot faster than they're going up.

It's Our Duty to Save Their Doody

These days, it's estimated that only about forty-five hundred Baird's Tapirs are still out there. To help protect these beloved "mountain cows," we've partnered with the Houston Zoo, US Fish and Wildlife Service, Zoo New England, the IUCN SSC Tapir Specialist Group, Proyecto Tapir Nicaragua, Belize's Foundation for Wildlife Conservation, ProCAT, and the Costa Rica Wildlife Foundation, and others. Together, we combine our resources and continue to find new ways to safeguard tapirs, their nutrient-filled poop, and, ultimately, entire ecosystems.

underfrog ● fact ●

Tapirs are one of the most "primitive" large mammals on Earth, meaning they've barely changed in the last thirty-five *million* years!

Baird's Tapir female with calf, Corcovado National Park, Costa Rica. Photo © Nick Hawkins

YELLOW-SHOULDERED PARROT

Animal: Yellow-Shouldered Parrot, aka Yellow-Shouldered Amazon

Class: Aves (Bird)

Species: *Amazona barbadensis*

Status: Vulnerable

Population Trend: Unknown

It's time for another conservation success story, starring the Yellow-Shouldered Parrot! This practically neon green and yellow cutie-pie is native to northern Venezuela and its islands of Margarita and La Blanquilla, as well as Bonaire, an island off the coast of Venezuela (though it is a municipality of the Netherlands).

Unlike most other little birdies in its genus, the Yellow-Shouldered Parrot, or Yellow-Shouldered Amazon—you say *poh-tAY-to*, we say *poh-tAH-to*—has a yellow shoulder patch and lots of yellow on its head. Other species of *Amazona* usually have red or orange on their shoulders and less-bright yellow heads.

Poached for Pets

The Yellow-Shouldered Parrot's gorgeous coloring makes it popular in the pet trade. It also has to deal with all the devastation that comes from habitat destruction, courtesy of human development.

Parrots and Provita

Most of the conservation efforts dedicated to protecting the Yellow-Shouldered Parrot have been led by species savior extraordinaire Dr. Jon Paul Rodríguez. Dr. Rodríguez serves as chair of the IUCN SSC and has been working in conservation for over thirty years now. When Jon Paul

(continued) ▶

Yellow-Shouldered Parrot, Echo Dos Pos Conservation Centre, Bonaire, Caribbean Netherlands. Photo © John C. Mittermeier

first pulled up to Margarita Island in search of the Yellow-Shouldered Parrot, there were only about 650 of them left. Dr. Rodríguez cofounded Provita, a long-term program protecting Yellow-Shouldered Parrot nests from poaching, and, thanks to them, the bird's wild population has since shot up to around seventeen hundred! Provita accomplished this by recruiting former poachers to become eco-guardians and maintain round-the-clock watch on the nests. These eco-guardians also helped to get local communities invested in the future of this fabulous color splotch of a bird! Their work eventually earned Dr. Rodríguez and his devoted team a Whitley Fund for Nature Award, aka a Green Oscar, and more importantly, restored hope for the Yellow-Shouldered Parrot.

underfrog fact

The Yellow-Shouldered Parrot is very friendly and outspoken and usually hangs out in flocks of up to a hundred birds.

ANDEAN CAT

Animal: Andean Cat
Class: Mammalia (Mammal)
Species: *Leopardus jacobita*
Status: Endangered
Population Trend: Decreasing

With fewer than twenty-five hundred thought to remain in the wild, the Andean Cat is just about the cutest little endangered species there is. Twice as large as your everyday house cat, this cuddly-looking bean prefers to live life more untamed. It hangs out up high in the Andes, pouncing from rock to rock and feeding on small mammals, small birds, waterfowl, and lizards. It even has an important spiritual significance—it's considered sacred by the Indigenous Aymara and Quechua peoples, bringing with it rich harvests, abundance and fertility of livestock, and even the transfer of supernatural powers to hunters. Before 1998, scientists didn't know very much about the Andean Cat, except that it existed. However, due to the hard work of conservationists, it's now one of the better-known small cats.

Heavily Hunted, Less Habitat

The Andean Cat has many threats working against it. First, there's habitat destruction and fragmentation caused by an overload of mining. And like we said earlier, the Andean Cat is sacred to some. Because of this, it's sometimes hunted for use in spiritual ceremonies. It's also hunted in northern Patagonia because farmers don't want it snatching up their livestock. To make matters even worse, its main prey—the Mountain Vizcacha—is also now heavily hunted, leaving our poor Andean Cat without its most important meal!

(continued) ▶

Finding the Feline

In 1998, Re:wild's program manager of wild cat conservation, Dr. Jim Sanderson, decided to go off and see if he could find the elusive feline himself after there had only ever been two sightings of it. For six weeks, Dr. Sanderson camped out on a rocky hillside and scanned the scene for the Andean kitty. Then one morning—like any other morning, except different—Jim stepped out of his campsite and BOOM! There it was, sitting just a mere 100 feet (30 meters) away!

The Andean Cat Renaissance

Since the rediscovery, a sort of Andean Cat renaissance has begun. Dr. Sanderson, a fellow of the Wildlife Conservation Network, founded the Andean Cat Alliance—which includes a team of scientists from all over the world. These organizations have set up a list of long-term goals and actions to help the Andean Cat thrive as a species. Thanks to Jim and his team, hopefully their curiosity will, ultimately, save the cat!

underfrog ●
fact ●

Before 1998, the Andean Cat had only been photographed twice!

Andean Cat, camera trap image, Chile.
Photo © Cristian Sepúlveda C.

ARAPAIMA

Animal: Arapaima, aka Paiche, or Pirarucu
Class: Actinopterygii (Fish)
Species: *Arapaima gigas*
Status: Data Deficient
Population Trend: Unspecified

They can be up to 15 feet (4.6 meters) long, 400 pounds (181 kilograms), and are some of the largest and oldest freshwater fish in the world. Called "the cod of the Amazon," the Arapaima is truly an ancient beast. These giants live in South America's Amazon Basin and some nearby lakes and swamps. Its bright red caudal fin earns the Arapaima its Brazilian name, *Pirarucu*, which roughly translates to "red fish" in the Tupi language.

Arapaima are known for being gill-less, air-breathing fish—they can only stay underwater for about 10–20 minutes before having to come up for air! Because of this, they tend to hang out toward the water's surface and use a modified swim bladder as a makeshift lung. The loud gulping sound they make as they "breathe" can be heard from very far away.

Catching and Cooking the Colossus

The Arapaima is super susceptible to being hunted by humans, especially if the humans are using harpoons or spears. Overfishing is a huge reason why the fish's numbers have fallen so dramatically. The Arapaima is considered an awesome "food fish" by locals since it's so rich in protein. Its meat can be stored without rotting, which is an added bonus in a region that doesn't have a whole lot of refrigeration. And since it's HUGE, this South American colossus is also seen as a prized trophy in Thailand's and Malaysia's sport fishing circles.

Careful Fishing

In the early 2000s, the Brazilian Institute of Environment and Renewable Natural Resources (aka IBAMA) tried out a new approach to conserve the Arapaima: co-management. This new system is all about collaboration between conservationists and fishing communities. It works like this: The fishers count the fish and work with IBAMA to set harvest quotas. This system also employs a lot of women, even though fishing in the Amazon is traditionally seen as an activity for fathers and sons. Though it might be a compromise, co-management is definitely helping everybody out, especially the Arapaima in the long run.

Arapaima, Amazon Basin, Brazil. Photo © Brandon Cole

underfrog ●
fact ●

The Arapaima have short bursts of incredible speed whereby they can propel themselves through the water to hunt their prey, but they can't keep up that speed for long. If they tire themselves out, they can sink and drown.

SANTA CATARINA'S GUINEA PIG

Animal: Santa Catarina's Guinea Pig
Class: Mammalia (Mammal)
Species: *Cavia intermedia*
Status: Critically Endangered
Population Trend: Decreasing

Santa Catarina's Guinea Pig is an *extremely* rare guinea pig species native to a teeny, tiny part of southeastern South America. Adding up to a measly 2.5 acres (or 0.01 square kilometer), this area has earned the Santa Catarina's Guinea Pig home range the superlative of "Smallest Geographic Range of Any Mammal." However, it's not like these little critters are overcrowding their minimal square footage—there are only an estimated forty individuals left. The fact that its numbers are in the double digits makes it one of the top twenty most threatened small mammals in the entire world.

This long-haired guinea pig was first discovered in 1999 in Serra do Tabuleiro State Park on Moleques do Sul Island in the state of Santa Catarina, Brazil. While this island is protected and entry isn't allowed, rules are not well enforced, which is bad news for our furry friend.

Close to *Meating* Its Fate

With its nearly microscopic population size and slow reproduction rate, Santa Catarina's Guinea Pig is in pretty hot water. Of course, when it comes to threats to this guinea pig's survival, habitat destruction is up there too, along with the very real possibility of getting gobbled up by the island's resident feral cats. At the end of the day, hunting (for its meat) is Santa Catarina's Guinea Pig's biggest threat.

Putting Together a Plan

Trying to get more of a grasp on these disappearing guinea pigs, one of Re:wild's partners, the IUCN SSC Small Mammal Specialist Group, is taking action. To learn more about this species, a team spent a year or so experimenting with capture-mark-recapture methods and radio telemetry, aka using radio signals to determine an animal's location. These days, they've put together an action plan to reduce negative impacts on the environment and educate local communities on this Critically Endangered furry animal.

underfrog ●
fact ●

Most—about 78 percent—Santa Catarina's Guinea Pigs give birth to only one offspring in a litter.

Santa Catarina's Guinea Pig, Moleques do Sul Island, Serra do Tabuleiro State Park, Brazil.
Photo © Luciano Candisani, Minden Pictures

FERNANDINA GALÁPAGOS TORTOISE

Animal: Fernandina Galápagos Tortoise
Class: Reptilia (Reptile)
Species: *Chelonoidis phantasticus*

Status: Critically Endangered
Population Trend: Unknown
Last Seen: 1906

When asked about the probability of rediscovering the Fernandina Galápagos Tortoise, Himalayan mountaineering legend Eric Shipton once said that the odds "were at least better than those of finding a Yeti."

A Mysterious Scat Scouting

After some particularly curious poops were found in 1964, and a 2009 flyover reported seeing some

sort of tortoise-esque shape from the air, people began holding out hope that we'd find the Fernandina Tortoise once again.

Its First (Possible) Television Appearance

It wasn't until 2019 that the Galápagos National Park Directorate, the Galápagos Conservancy, and Animal Planet found a tortoise on Fernandina Island. While the tortoise *might* be a Fernandina Tortoise, Re:wild partners are using paternity testing to determine whether it is in fact the first individual of this species seen in over one hundred years, or a look-alike species that swam over from another island.

underfrog ● fact ●

The Fernandina Tortoise's biggest threat was—and continues to be—frequent volcanic eruptions.

SINÚ PARAKEET

Animal: Sinú Parakeet

Class: Aves (Bird)

Species: *Pyrrhura subandina*

Status: Critically Endangered

Population Trend: Decreasing

Last Seen: 1949

This gorgeous rainbow-splattered bird is none other than the Sinú Parakeet, named after its home Sinú Valley in northern Colombia. The Sinú Parakeet is another one of our 25 Most Wanted Lost Species. While no one's seen this parakeet since 1949, we're still holding on to hope—after all, some researchers say that if it's not Extinct, there are probably around fifty of them still left on Earth.

Protect the Parakeet!

With more and more of its habitat destroyed for agriculture, the Sinú Parakeet's range has drastically shrunk from what it once was. Not much is known about the bird's diet, ecology, or behavior, but hopefully with more in-depth surveying, we will not only rediscover the Sinú Parakeet, but also be able to learn more about how to better care for it and its home in the future!

underfrog ● fact ●

Everything that scientists know about the Sinú Parakeet has come from the only seventeen individuals that have ever been sighted in four locations in Colombia. Unfortunately, two of those places have now been deforested.

ESTEBAN BRENES-MORA

Name: Esteban Brenes-Mora
Tapir Expert
Title: Founder and Director of Nai Conservation
Organization: Costa Rica Wildlife Foundation

When Esteban Brenes-Mora was a kid, his grandpa showed him pictures and told him all sorts of stories about Mesoamerican animals. Then when he was five, he saw his first tapir—that was the moment that changed *everything*! After that, Esteban went on to study biology and completely committed himself to all things tapir.

Today, Esteban is the founder and director of Nai Conservation, a group of young, diverse researchers working to save tapir populations and their habitat in Costa Rica. Esteban has been fighting against tapir threats for about six years now. He's developed roadkill mitigation measures and anti-poaching strategies, and continues to work with local farmers to promote tapir-friendly agriculture and develop tapir ecotourism!

Besides leading Nai Conservation, Esteban also works as one of Re:wild's associate conservation scientists and as part of the Baird's Tapir Survival Alliance. Thanks to Esteban and his team, the Endangered Baird's Tapir has a chance at a better and more secure future in Costa Rica!

Esteban Brenes-Mora, founder and director of Nai Conservation. Photo © Nick Hawkins

TERESA CAMACHO BADANI

Name: Teresa Camacho Badani
Bolivian Amphibian Expert (and Frog Matchmaker)
Title: Chief Herpetologist
Organization: Museo de Historia Natural Alcide d'Orbigny/Centro K'ayra

When it comes to love stories, there are very few that are as romantic as that of Romeo the Frog! It all started when the Centro K'ayra at the Museo de Historia Natural Alcide d'Orbigny began caring for Romeo, the last-known Sehuencas Water Frog. With no potential mates ever showing up, poor Romeo eventually started to give up hope. It was then that Re:wild offered to help find Romeo a mate. So, we made Romeo a Match.com dating profile!

Through our partnership with the world's largest relationship company, we were able to raise $25,000 to send an expedition team into the Bolivian mountains to look for Romeo's mate. That's where Teresa Camacho Badani and her team come in. In addition to caring for Romeo, they also planned expeditions in search of a love for their lonely frog. And on one expedition, Lady Luck *finally* came and found her! Of course, the team simply *had* to name the female Sehuencas Water Frog Juliet.

Now the team is caring for Romeo, Juliet, and their friends, and keeping their fingers (and toes) crossed for tadpoles. Thanks to Teresa, the entire Sehuencas Water Frog species has a chance to keep on keepin' on!

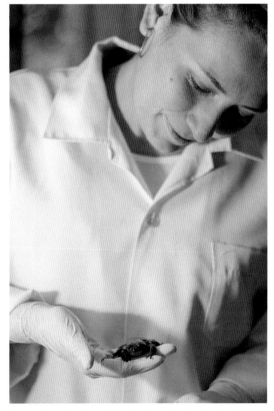

Teresa Camacho Badani, head of herpetology, Centro K'ayra, Museo de Historia Natural Alcide d'Orbigny, Bolivia.
Photo © Robin Moore, Re:wild

6

Oceana

TUATARA

Animal: Tuatara
Class: Reptilia (Reptile)
Species: *Sphenodon punctatus*
Status: Least Concern
Population Trend: Unknown

Clocking in at almost 2 feet (61 centimeters), this scaly New Zealander is the country's largest reptile—it's the Tuatara! The Tuatara is the only surviving member of the order Rhynchocephalia, which rubbed elbows with the dinosaurs millions of years ago. All other Rhynchocephalians eventually went Extinct. All but the Tuatara.

Tuatara is a word that comes from the Indigenous people of New Zealand, the Māori, and roughly translates to "peaks on back" or "spiny back." This mostly nocturnal reptile got its name for the crests on its back, called spines, that run all the way down its tail. In addition, the Tuatara has the lowest optimal body temperature of any reptile.

Tuatara in Trouble

When the first humans arrived in New Zealand, they were welcomed by hordes of Tuatara. But the people brought with them some unwelcome guests—rats and dogs—both of which would make a meal out of Tuatara eggs and Tuatara babies. Later, European settlers came to New Zealand and added cats, stoats, and ferrets to the list of invasive predators. Prior to human settlement, the Tuatara lived on New Zealand's North and South Islands, in addition to a number of the country's smaller offshore islands, with a population in the millions. Today, it only lives in the wild on offshore islands, where invasive predators are not an issue.

(continued) ▶

Tuatara, North Brother Island, New Zealand.
Photo © Frans Lanting/www.lanting.com

A New Headstart

The Tuatara was actually the first-ever species fully protected by New Zealand law in 1895. Nearly a century later, in 1988, the New Zealand Department of Conservation launched a recovery program for the Tuatara (though extensive conservation efforts had already begun). Biologists raised hatchlings until they were big enough to survive in the wild on their own, a process called "headstarting." They then released the Tuatara onto islands free of invasive species, and that's where this dinosaur-adjacent reptile remains today.

underfrog ● fact ●

The Tuatara has a "third eye" on top of its head! This eye, called a parietal eye, has a retina and lens, but the Tuatara doesn't actually use it for seeing. Since this mysterious parietal eye is so sensitive to light, researchers think it may be used to help the Tuatara figure out what time of day or season it is.

KAKĪ

Animal: Kakī, aka Black Stilt
Class: Aves (Bird)
Species: *Himantopus novaezelandiae*
Status: Critically Endangered
Population Trend: Increasing

The Black Stilt, or Kakī in the Māori language—once called New Zealand's "Common Stilt"—is now the rarest wading bird in the world. Back in 1981, it was *so* rare that there were only twenty-three known birds left on the entire planet. With its black feathers, red eyes, and long skinny red legs, it definitely is a cute-yet-gothic sight to behold! The Māori people are well aware of just how special this bird is. In their language, they call it a *taonga*, which roughly translates to a "living treasure."

Flight, but No Fight

The Kakī *can* fly away from introduced predators like feral cats and ferrets, but because of changes to the bird's habitat, the predators have ample opportunities to hide and then pounce on the unsuspecting birds. A lot of hydroelectric dams and farms have also been constructed in the Kakī's wetland habitat. When humans go out into the Kakī's domain, they can also step on eggs and chicks, or just scare adult Kakī away from their nests.

Very, Very Aviary

Thanks to New Zealand's Department of Conservation (DOC), the world's rarest wading bird is set to make a comeback! Along with other nonprofits, landowners, and Māori communities, Re:wild is helping to support DOC's wildly successful conservation breeding and reintroduction programs. A lot of this success has relied on the six-bay aviaries that give young Kakī a

(continued) ▶

safe place to grow before they head back to the wild. In 2015, a huge snowstorm rolled through and destroyed one of the aviaries and severely damaged another. With funding from Re:wild, thanks to the generous support of the Sheth Sangreal Foundation, DOC was able to build a second hand-rearing facility and a bigger, better ten-bay aviary that increased the program's rearing capacity by at least sixty chicks per year. All the work up to this point has bolstered the Kakī population from a measly twenty-three back in the 1980s to over 170 in the wild today, and thanks to these new aviaries, that number will only continue to go up!

underfrog ● fact ●

Just a couple hours after hatching, Kakī chicks are already raring to go out and hunt for their own food!

Kakī, South Island, New Zealand.
Photo © Liz Brown, Department of Conservation

NORTHERN BROWN KIWI

Animal: Northern Brown Kiwi, aka Brown Kiwi
Class: Aves (Bird)
Species: *Apteryx mantelli*
Status: Vulnerable
Population Trend: Stable

You may have heard people from New Zealand call themselves "kiwis"—well, that's because of their pride in the Kiwi! The feathers of this iconic and endemic bird are so sacred to the Māori, the Indigenous people of New Zealand, that the feathers of Kiwi living abroad in zoos are often sent back to them.

Not only is this downy-feathered, long-beaked species considered sacred; it has also been called an "honorary mammal"—in other words, a total biological weirdo. The Northern Brown Kiwi is nocturnal, it can't fly, and it holds the world record for the land bird that lays the largest egg in proportion to its body size. To put this into perspective, the egg takes up nearly the entirety of the female's abdomen.

Some Sad Stats

As far as threats go, the Northern Brown Kiwi mostly faces invasive predators such as dogs, cats, ferrets, and stoats (a weasel-like small mammal). According to some reports, a single dog once killed over five hundred Kiwi in one incident. It's estimated that only about 5 percent of Kiwi live to be adults.

Who Ya Gonna Call? Pest Control!

Active pest management has made a huge difference in how many Northern Brown Kiwi chicks make it to adulthood. Since invasive predator removal programs were first introduced, the number of adult Kiwi birds in New Zealand's Tongariro Forest has—thankfully—doubled. And even though living near humans can come with risks, like dogs, cats, and cars, it also has a silver lining. Today, lots of these neighboring communities are starting their own initiatives to help save their country's most iconic bird. Got to love kiwis helping the Kiwi!

underfrog ●
fact ●

Northern Brown Kiwi are monogamous, though "divorces"
are known to happen on occasion.

Northern Brown Kiwi in human care, North Island, New Zealand. Photo © Roland Seitre, Nature Picture Library

SOUTHERN CORROBOREE FROG

Animal: Southern Corroboree Frog
Class: Amphibia (Amphibian)
Species: *Pseudophryne corroboree*
Status: Critically Endangered
Population Trend: Decreasing

The Southern Corroboree Frog is one of Australia's most endangered species. With its bright yellow and black stripes, and the occasional blue belly, it's one of the most beautiful and legendary animals on the entire continent. But they're a lot more than just a pretty face—Southern Corroboree Frogs are also superstars within Australia's alpine ecosystems.

These neon-colored amphibians live exclusively in Kosciuszko National Park, where they're found chilling at altitudes above 4,000 feet (1,300 meters). Up there, their tadpoles devour any and all algae in the ponds, which ultimately keeps the water crystal clear and the aquatic plants and animals happy.

Pretty 'n' Poisonous

While their bright colors and bold patterns make them one of the world's most recognizable frogs, there is a method to this evolutionary madness— their colors indicate that there are poisonous alkaloids in their skin. This protects them from predation. Thanks to this deadly adaptation, the Southern Corroboree Frog actually has no known predators.

Chytrid-Proofing

This little froggy's primary threats are climate change, fires, habitat destruction, and, sometimes, feral animals, which destroy its breeding grounds by trampling the habitat. But in more recent years, its *biggest* threat has become the deadly invasive chytrid fungus, which has wiped out entire frog species across Australia, Latin America, and the western United States. Chytrid quickly spreads from frog to frog and has killed off entire species, while pushing others to the brink of extinction.

Kiddie Pools for Conservation

With the species' numbers declining since the mid-1980s, researchers think there might only be around fifty adult Southern Corroborees left in the wild. Luckily, a number of organizations in Australia have launched conservation breeding programs to help. These programs release Southern Corroboree Frog eggs back into the wild. The eggs are released mostly into artificial pools designed to keep out the chytrid fungus and protect the frogs from droughts. It takes four to five years for the frogs to reach adulthood, so we're not sure yet if the released eggs will develop into fully mature frogs who will then breed. But with all of these forward-thinking efforts in place, the Southern Corroboree Frog seems to have a chance!

underfrog ● fact ●

The Southern Corroboree Frog is nocturnal but will sometimes make an appearance during the day if it's just dark and cloudy enough.

Southern Corroboree Frog, twenty years ago in Kosciuszko National Park, Australia.
Photo © Pavel German

SOUTH ISLAND TAKAHĒ

Animal: South Island Takahē
Class: Aves (Bird)
Species: *Porphyrio hochstetteri*
Status: Endangered
Population Trend: Increasing

There's no other way to say it—the South Island Takahē is one wild-looking bird. It has a bright red beak, red legs, and a blue and iridescent green body that looks kind of peacock-ish. This is the world's largest member of the rail family, a group of birds that can't fly, so its stature isn't exactly *aerodynamic*. While it may be flightless, the takahē sure ain't wingless! It uses its wings to attract potential partners (hubba hubba!) and to show aggression when it needs to.

Native to New Zealand, the takahē has cultural, spiritual, and traditional significance to Ngāi Tahu, the Indigenous Māori *iwi* (or tribe) of most of the South Island. The South Island Takahē was actually thought to be Extinct for about fifty years but was (fortunately!) rediscovered in 1948.

No Flight = No Fight

Like a lot of other flightless birds, invasive predators have shown the South Island Takahē no mercy. Habitat destruction and competition over food—mostly with deer—also hasn't helped.

What's more, takahē are slow breeders. Normally, they only have one to two chicks each year. These stats *definitely* mean it's going to take a while for them to bounce back. In 2020, the estimated South Island Takahē population was almost 450 birds.

Numbers Going Up in the (Gouland) Downs

There is an upside, though—the rediscovery of the lost South Island Takahē launched New Zealand's longest-running endangered species program! For over seventy years, the country's Department of Conservation (DOC) has been working with Māori tribes and a team of scientists to develop and run conservation breeding programs, implement monitoring methods, do island translocations and releases, and explore invasive species control options. The ultimate goal of DOC's Takahē Recovery Programme is returning South Island Takahē to the wild.

In 2018, the team was finally able to reintroduce thirty South Island Takahē back onto

South Island Takahē, Te Anau Bird Sanctuary, New Zealand. Photo © Anja Köhler

Gouland Downs in Kahurangi National Park, with the hope of establishing a second wild population. The majority of the birds have survived —and some breeding has been going on. The team's next goal? Find more safe homes to establish additional wild populations in the native grasslands of the South Island!

underfrog ● fact ●

The South Island Takahē's closest relative, the North Island Takahē, or *moho*, in the Māori language, is sadly, *actually* Extinct.

TASMANIAN DEVIL

Animal: Tasmanian Devil
Class: Mammalia (Mammal)
Species: *Sarcophilus harrisii*
Status: Endangered
Population Trend: Decreasing

We're sure you're familiar with Taz the Tasmanian Devil from the Looney Tunes Show, a cartoon icon in his own right. But the real Tasmanian Devil is even *more* iconic—this famously depicted species is known for being the world's largest carnivorous marsupial still around today! Adults usually weigh anywhere between 11 and 30 pounds (5 and 14 kilograms) and can grow to be about 2 feet (61 centimeters) long.

The Tasmanian Devil will eat just about anything (dead or alive!) as long as it's an animal, from insects to amphibians to birds and mammals. This furry, innocent-looking teddy bear is even known to dabble in cannibalism from time to time.

The Devil's Disease

The Tasmanian Devil could once be found on both Tasmania and mainland Australia, but Dingoes and, more recently, Devil Facial Tumor Disease, a contagious cancer devils spread through bites to the face, have just about wiped this species out. The devil was completely Extinct on Australia's mainland until 2020, when our close partner Aussie Ark, with Re:wild's support, released twenty-six to a wild sanctuary in Barrington Tops. It was the first time Tasmanian Devils had lived in the wild on mainland Australia in three thousand years. In Tasmania, the Tasmanian Devil's population is now less than 10 percent of what it once was. If a Tasmanian Devil escapes Devil Facial Tumor Disease, it still has to dodge becoming roadkill or lunch for dogs and foxes.

(continued) ▶

Tasmanian Devil, Aussie Ark, Australia.
Photo © David Stowe Photography/www.davidstowe.com

"State-of-the-Ark" Conservation

In 2011, Aussie Ark established a "state-of-the-ark" conservation facility to breed baby Tazzies. Researchers believe that Tasmanian Devils could help bring back historically functional ecosystems by returning to their natural role as apex predator and scavenger in the forests of Australia. In this highly coveted role, the Tasmanian Devil would help keep the number of invasive foxes and cats in check. Since starting this program, Aussie Ark has overseen the births of more than three hundred Tasmanian Devil joeys, making it the world's biggest, most successful, and most economical Tasmanian Devil breeding program!

underfrog
fact

The Tasmanian Devil has a short life span. They can live up to five or six years in the wild, and about eight years in human care.

LONG-NOSED POTOROO

Animal: Long-Nosed Potoroo
Class: Mammalia (Mammal)
Species: *Potorous tridactylus*
Status: Near Threatened
Population Trend: Decreasing

Holding the title of one of the smallest and most ancient members of the kangaroo family, the Long-Nosed Potoroo is called a living fossil, which means it has remained basically unchanged for around ten million years!

It looks like a giant mouse or a bandicoot, which it is mistaken for more often than not. While this marsupial usually just waddles around, the potoroo's only real kangaroo-esque quality—besides having a pouch, of course—is that it hops away when it's scared. The Long-Nosed Potoroo could once be found in every corner of southeastern Australia, but these days, that's not so much the case.

Developments, Destruction, and Other Dangers

Clearing land for agriculture and buildings has destroyed a lot of important potoroo habitat. This also undermines the health of the whole ecosystem by splitting up Long-Nosed Potoroo populations. Like many of its other marsupial friends, the Long-Nosed Potoroo has to watch out for predators like foxes and cats.

Protecting the Potoroo

The potoroo is one of the seven eco-engineers that Aussie Ark is helping out in their "exclosures," high-tech, predator-free outdoor conservation breeding facilities. Aussie Ark, a close

(continued) ▷

partner of Re:wild, is also doing everything they can to protect the Long-Nosed Potoroo's habitat. On their ground sites, Aussie Ark removes and manages stock and feral herbivores, which, in turn, protects vegetation, prevents forest fires, and gets invasive predators to back off. Currently, Aussie Ark is trying to build up a conservation breeding population that they can release back into the wilds of Australia.

underfrog
fact

The Long-Nosed Potoroo is basically the firefighter of Australia's wilderness—by grazing undergrowth and turning over leaf litter that would otherwise be kindling, the potoroo does its part to reduce the chance of forest fires!

Long-Nosed Potoroo, Aussie Ark, Australia.
Photo © Aussie Ark

EASTERN QUOLL

Animal: Eastern Quoll
Class: Mammalia (Mammal)
Species: *Dasyurus viverrinus*
Status: Endangered
Population Trend: Decreasing

A close relative of the legendary Tasmanian Tiger, the Eastern Quoll looks more like a big, fuzzy rodent. These medium-sized marsupials were once scattered all over Australia but were officially declared Extinct on the mainland in 1963. It has spots kind of like a baby deer and a bushy tail that may or may not have a little white tip. It also comes in two colors: a gingery brown or deep black, both color options topped off with the spots. Long story short, it's pretty freakin' cute!

The Eastern Quoll is a key species when it comes to the checks and balances of ecosystems. Its specialty is scouring the forest floor for small animals, playing the role of natural predator.

A Wake-Up Quoll

Habitat destruction, trapping, and the introduction of non-native species—namely cats and foxes—have been a huge danger to the Eastern Quoll population. It's estimated that there are around ten thousand Eastern Quolls left in Tasmania, but numbers are quickly falling.

From the Ark to the Park

Since 2017, our friends at Aussie Ark—along with some help from Re:wild and other organizations—have been rebuilding a population of quolls at their 1,200-acre (22–square kilometer) wildlife sanctuary in northern New South Wales. In the spring of 2019, Aussie Ark released seventeen of their sixty-nine captive-bred Eastern Quolls out into Australia's Booderee National Park. This marked the first-ever successful release of captive-bred quolls, and the second-ever release of quolls onto the mainland. The first release took place the year before, also in Booderee, and we are happy to report that those Eastern Quolls are now making babies!

underfrog ● fact ●

The Eastern Quoll is a carnivore, eating spiders, cockroaches, grasshoppers, rabbits, mice, and rats.

Eastern Quoll, Aussie Ark, Australia.
Photo © David Stowe Photography/www.davidstowe.com

KĀKĀPŌ

Animal: Kākāpō
Class: Aves (Bird)
Species: *Strigops habroptilus*
Status: Critically Endangered
Population Trend: Increasing

The Kākāpō kind of looks like what you'd get if a parakeet mated with a pheasant, and then you sprinkled in a hint of owl. If that doesn't already paint a weird enough picture, this bird is also nocturnal, it can't fly, and it holds the title of world's heaviest parrot. Did we mention it's quite possibly the world's most ancient bird?

This feathered enigma has called New Zealand home for millions of years. In its forests, the Kākāpō happily lives a mostly solitary life. While each individual Kākāpō has its own unique personality—some can be super friendly and playful, while others are total grumps—some behaviors are universal. For example, all Kākāpō are pretty slow-but-steady hikers, and they all rely on the tactic of standing completely still whenever they feel threatened.

Oh No, Not the Kākāpō!

On New Zealand's Rakiura/Stewart Island in the 1980s, about 50 percent of monitored adult Kākāpō were killed by cats every year. Recently, introduced species like stoats and rats have also become a major problem. Polynesian Rats sweep in and eat the bird's young. Today the only safe place for the Kākāpō is predator-free islands.

Give It Up for the Kākāpō Recovery Program!

Back in 2007, there were only eighty-five Kākāpō left on our great green planet. Thanks to our partner, the New Zealand Department of Conservation (DOC), the Kākāpō population is now hanging out in the two hundreds. Since establishing the Kākāpō Recovery Programme back in 1995—when the Kākāpō population was at its all-time lowest of just fifty-one individuals—DOC and its volunteers have worked nonstop to monitor this rather robust parrot and reduce its population threats. Today, the Kākāpō lives and breeds on three of New Zealand's remote, predator-free islands: Whenua Hou (Codfish Island), Anchor Island, and Hauturu-o-Toi (Little Barrier Island).

Kākāpō, Codfish Island/Whenua Hou, New Zealand. Photo © Jake Osborne, Department of Conservation

underfrog
fact

The Kākāpō gives off a sweet scent that's often
compared to honey.

BRUSH-TAILED ROCK WALLABY

Animal: Brush-Tailed Rock Wallaby
Class: Mammalia (Mammal)
Species: *Petrogale penicillata*
Status: Vulnerable
Population Trend: Decreasing

Nestled in the quaint and cozy rock piles and cliff lines along Australia's Great Dividing Range, the Brush-Tailed Rock Wallaby lives a quiet, yet rewarding life with these mountains as the backdrop. This mammal's trademark feature is its brush tail namesake, which helps the Brush-Tailed Rock Wallaby keep its balance as it bounds from rock to rock. It was also blessed with strong legs, claws, and padded feet that allow it to climb up even the most vertical cliffs.

While its range has significantly declined, this mountain-dwelling macropod can still be found from southeastern Queensland all the way to Western Victoria. Heads up, though, it might be hard to see—the Brush-Tailed Rock Wallaby's brown and gray body is great camouflage in its rocky habitat!

A Rocky Reality

Life hasn't been the easiest for our dear old rock wallaby friend. Much of its habitat has been destroyed by forest fires, exotic plant invasions, and the general clearing of native vegetation. These threats have slowly but surely nudged the Brush-Tailed Rock Wallaby out of the southern and western corners of its range. Introduced predators (foxes) and environmental competitors (wild goats, sheep, and rabbits) also haven't given the wallaby any breaks. Wait, there's more: In the past, the Brush-Tailed Rock Wallaby was considered a pest and was hunted and skinned for its pelt.

(continued) ▶

Brush-Tailed Rock Wallaby, Aussie Ark, Australia.
Photo © Aussie Ark

Rewilding the Rock Wallaby

The Brush-Tailed Rock Wallaby is one of the seven species our partner Aussie Ark is working to rewild. As of today, fewer than twenty thousand of these marsupials are left in the wild, with as few as ten in some fragmented populations. Aussie Ark has started building a predator-free sanctuary for the Brush-Tailed Rock Wallaby. By 2021, Aussie Ark believes they'll have over thirty-five Brush-Tailed Rock Wallabies thriving in their care—this way, they'll be off to a great start for establishing a glowing insurance population.

underfrog ●
fact ●

The Brush–Tailed Rock Wallaby has some distinct facial markings, namely a white stripe on each of its cheeks and a long black streak that runs from its forehead to the back of its head.

LORD HOWE ISLAND STICK INSECT

Animal: Lord Howe Island Stick Insect, aka Tree Lobster
Class: Insecta (Insect)
Species: *Dryococelus australis*
Status: Critically Endangered
Population Trend: Unknown

Nicknamed the Tree Lobster, the Lord Howe Island Stick Insect perfectly fits that analogy. This 4-inch-long (10-centimeter-long) black bug has the same exoskeletal look as its aquatic counterpart, and a mysterious seafaring past to go with it!

These guys were once so plentiful on Lord Howe Island (a small island more than 350 miles [563 kilometers] off the coast of Australia) that fisherpeople would use them as bait. But after a ship wrecked on the island in 1918 and released rats that dispersed across it, the species quickly started disappearing—by the early 1920s, it was considered to be Extinct. But then in 1960 and several times in the following decades—HUZZAH!—a group of rock climbers miraculously found recently deceased Tree Lobsters on a small, rocky sea stack 14 miles (23 kilometers)

from the main island! However, their survival wasn't *officially* confirmed by scientists until 2001, when live animals were found.

I Don't Want No Shrubs

Because the Tree Lobster's population is so small and is only found on a single small volcanic island, it's pretty safe to say that this stick bug species *isn't* safe from any random or unpredictable disaster. Droughts, storms, and even an invasive vine species called *Ipomoea cairica* pose threats to this stick insect's survival. This vine is especially scary since it could lead to the death of *Melaleuca*, the shrub that the Tree Lobster depends on for food, shelter, and just general survival.

(continued) ▶

Un-Sticking This Stick Bug

Realizing that this stick bug was about to be *stuck*, several zoos decided to "adopt" a bunch of its eggs. Eggs were flown to Melbourne Zoo, and once the conservation breeding program showed success, additional eggs were flown to California, Bristol, and Toronto to get more breeding programs up and running. Today, there are about seven hundred individuals and thousands upon thousands of Tree Lobster eggs in the Melbourne Zoo's program alone.

In addition to a conservation breeding program, folks got to work removing invasive plants from the Tree Lobster's habit in 2003, and successfully removed those pesky rats and mice from Lord Howe Island in 2019. Once all this is said and done, we hope the Lord Howe Island Stick Insect is going to have one helluva reintroduction!

underfrog
fact

An adult female Lord Howe Island Stick Insect is about the size of an adult human hand.

Lord Howe Island Stick Insect, Zoos Victoria, Australia.
Photo © Rohan Cleave, Zoos Victoria

AUSTRALIAN LUNGFISH

Animal: Australian Lungfish, aka Queensland Lungfish
Class: Sarcopterygii (Fish)
Species: *Neoceratodus forsteri*
Status: Endangered
Population Trend: Stable

The Australian Lungfish is set apart from most other fish by its ability to breathe with a lung, which means it breathes air! The Australian Lungfish only uses this lung when it really needs to, like when streams become stagnant during dry spells and dissolved oxygen in the water drops to dangerous levels. In the fish world, this is basically a superpower and has ensured lungfish have survived since the time of dinosaurs.

The Australian Lungfish—also called the Queensland Lungfish—was first documented back in 1870. Native to deep, slow-flowing freshwater pools in southeastern Queensland, the Australian Lungfish is known for its long, heavy body with big scales, its paddle-like pectoral and pelvic fins, and its tiny eyes.

Dam, That Sucks

When it comes to survival, dams and any other activity barriers that change the natural course of a river are the Australian Lungfish's number one concern. This air-breathing, omnivorous fish relies on what's called a "complex underwater habitat," which is basically just pools full of woody debris, shade, and aquatic plants that are good for spawning, shelter, and foraging. Degradation of this kind of habitat is caused by water storage, land use changes, and erosion, just to name a few. The lungfish's very specific breeding requirements (shallow water, dense macrophyte cover, and so on) also limit its options when dams are a part of the picture, and has meant that very few baby lungfish have been seen since the species was first discovered.

The Proposal We've Been Waiting For

Fortunately, the Australian Lungfish is a protected species, and a specialized permit is needed if someone wants to hunt it. Strict regulations are also in place to prevent people from exporting the fish. While no official recovery plan is currently set in stone, one has been proposed and is just waiting for the green light. The plan recommends reducing the impact from dams and other barriers by providing environmental flows, improving water quality, and rehabilitating lungfish breeding spots immediately following floods.

underfrog ●
fact ●

When the Australian Lungfish surfaces to breathe, the sound it makes has been compared to "a small blast from the bellows." The Australian Lungfish can also live for more than one hundred years!

Australian Lungfish, Mary River, Australia.
Photo © Liz Harlin, Undersea Productions

MANNING RIVER TURTLE

Animal: Manning River Turtle, aka Manning River Sawshelled Turtle, Purvis' Turtle
Class: Reptilia (Reptile)
Species: *Myuchelys purvisi* (many of its friends also use the alternative name *Wollumbinia purvisi*)
Status: Data Deficient
Population Trend: Unspecified

The Manning River Turtle is easy to spot, thanks to its bright yellow stripes and markings. It can only be found in the middle and upper parts of the Manning River in Australia's New South Wales, where it prefers shallow, clear, and constantly fast-flowing rivers with luxurious rocky and sandy beds. During the day, this reptile can often be found basking on nearby rocks, but by night, it's a mysterious nocturnal forager!

Wildfires and Other Worries

Habitat destruction (mostly due to cattle farming for beef), disease, and fire are the major threats that this shelled species faces. In October of 2019, wildfires tore through Australia, destroying tens of thousands of acres and homes in its wake. Fortunately, when it finally rained, oh, it RAINED. That February, torrential downpours unleashed the floodgates for, well, floods. While these floods put out the fire, they also presented brand-new problems—especially for aquatic reptiles like the Manning River Turtle. Many turtles were displaced from their homes, which made them more vulnerable to predators. Ash and soil washed into the rivers, polluting them and the vegetation and animals living there.

Trailblazing Turts

In 2017, Re:wild's close partner Aussie Ark came together with the Australian Reptile Park to propose the world's first-ever conservation breeding program for the Manning River Turtle. These organizations launched a month-long crowdfunding campaign that ended up being very successful—helping build facilities to establish an insurance population of the species. In early 2020, the breeding program hatched its first turtle babies. These teeny, tiny, adorable Manning River Turtle hatchlings now get to enjoy this new specialized facility, complete with all sorts of ponds, nurseries, and incubators. It's basically a five-star turtle hotel!

Looking to the future, Aussie Ark and the Australian Reptile Park plan on establishing an assurance population of twenty founding turtles and then releasing two hundred to three hundred juvenile turtles back into Manning River every year!

underfrog ● fact ●

The Manning River Turtle is believed to be an omnivore, eating both plants and animals. And while you may think that a turtle is too slow to catch prey by pursuing it at speed (and you'd be right about that), the Manning River Turtle instead surprises small animals as it forages between rocks and tree roots.

Manning River Turtle being rescued by Aussie Ark during the bushfire season, Australia. Photo © Aussie Ark

CHRISTMAS ISLAND SHREW

Animal: Christmas Island Shrew
Class: Mammalia (Mammal)
Species: *Crocidura trichura*

Status: Critically Endangered
Population Trend: Decreasing
Last Seen: 1985

Despite their "bad reputation" for associating with witches and even "turning wine sour," shrews are adorable and too often overlooked! Australia's only native shrew species, the Christmas Island Shrew, was once widespread and very common all over its namesake Indian Ocean island, but after the last sighting in the 1980s, this mammal is now one of Re:wild's most wanted lost small mammals. Because of human settlement from the 1880s, and the introduction of new predators and disease, the Christmas Island Shrew's numbers dramatically declined. By 1908, experts feared it was Extinct. However, two individuals were found in 1958 and another two in the 1980s, giving us some hope that this shrew may just be keeping a *very* low profile. This hope, unfortunately, is diminishing, as recent surveys (including searching for evidence of shrews in feral cat scat) have been unsuccessful at confirming that the shrew is still out there.

Waiting in the Wings

Keeping this hope alive and well, the Australian government has hatched a plan in case the Christmas Island Shrew actually is rediscovered. Until then, the Australian government is focusing on educating locals about the shrew and how to identify it.

underfrog ● fact ●

While the Christmas Island Shrew looks a lot like a long-nosed mouse, it's actually entirely unrelated to rodents.

SOUTH ISLAND KŌKAKO

Animal: South Island Kōkako

Class: Aves (Bird)

Species: *Callaeas cinerea*

Status: Critically Endangered

Population Trend: Decreasing

Last Seen: 2007

With a haunting call that has been compared to a cathedral bell and even a ghostly cry, the South Island Kōkako is one bizarre and beautiful ancient bird. It was last seen on New Zealand's South Island in 2007, which made headlines because the bird had been declared Extinct. Today the bird's status in New Zealand is Data Deficient.

The South Island Kōkako's sister species, the North Island Kōkako, has been brought back from the brink of extinction. Conservationists believe they can do the same if and when they do find this elusive southern counterpart.

A South Island Scavenger Hunt

The South Island Kōkako Charitable Trust is the only organization currently focused on this bird. They are urging people to keep their eyes (and ears!) open for the mysterious, secretive, and elusive species. The South Island Kōkako Charitable Trust keeps everyone updated on all the latest kōkako news and has developed an interactive map showing the location, date, and description of all reported possible encounters. This helps make finding this species feel a lot less daunting.

underfrog ●
fact ●

The main difference between the South and North Island Kōkako is that the North Island Kōkako has a blue wattle, while the South Island Kōkako's wattle varies from pale yellow to red.

JAKE OSBORNE

Name: Jake Osborne
Kākāpō Expert
Title: Kākāpō Ranger
Organization: New Zealand Department of Conservation

Like many other wildlife heroes, Jake Osborne began his foray into conservation through volunteering. He worked in a variety of roles with New Zealand's Department of Conservation (DOC) over three years, eventually landing a temporary contract with the Kākāpō Recovery team during the thick of the 2016 Kākāpō breeding season, and honestly, that's all it took for Jake—one season and he was hooked!

Soon after his stint with the Kākāpō team, Jake wasted no time and permanently joined the DOC. He took his post as a field ranger, where he now gets to work and live with Kākāpō for months at a time. If he's not busy catching the birds to give them checkups, maintaining equipment, or hand-rearing Kākāpō chicks, he's off photographing the birds and their gorgeous habitat out on pest-free islands around New Zealand.

Jake Osborne with Sirocco the Kākāpō, New Zealand. Photo © Sara Larcombe

While Jake says it can be hard to live away from home for so long, he feels incredibly lucky that he gets to work with such great friends and teammates, and of course, the legendary Kākāpō!

TIM FAULKNER

Name: Tim Faulkner
Australian Wildlife Expert
Title: President of Aussie Ark
Organization: Aussie Ark

Wrestling crocodiles, tagging wild platypuses, and even milking—yes, *milking*—Funnel-Web Spiders are just day-to-day activities for Tim Faulkner, the president of Re:wild partner Aussie Ark! Tim is THE Australian wildlife expert—he's dedicated his entire life to hands-on conservation and wildlife education. He stays busy running the Australian Reptile Park, the Central Coast's largest tourism attraction. If that's not enough, Tim also hosts his own TV show, *Outback Adventures with Tim Faulkner*. Because of everything he's accomplished for Australian wildlife, Tim was named 2015's Australian Geographic Conservationist of the Year!

At the end of the day, though, all of Tim's work comes down to his overwhelming love and passion for all of Australia's furry, spiky, and scaly species. On his own time, Tim serves as an ambassador and activist for many different animals, like the Tasmanian Devil, the Quokka, and the Dingo. He's even known to have little Aussie animals around, like baby Tasmanian Devils, or even a Wallaby just chillin' under his desk. Just another day in Tim's office!

Tim Faulkner, president of Aussie Ark, Australia.
Photo © Aussie Ark

Antarctica

ANTARCTIC MIDGE

Animal: Antarctic Midge
Class: Insecta (Insect)
Species: *Belgica antarctica*
Status: Unknown
Population Trend: Unknown

Only one insect in the entire world is able to survive at the bottom of our frigid planet—and that insect, friends, is the Antarctic Midge. The midge is also one of Antarctica's largest native land animals, though it is less than 0.4 inches (1 centimeter) long (this doesn't include marine-adapted animals like Leopard Seals and Emperor Penguins). And unlike all of the other animals in this book, the Antarctic Midge spends a good chunk of its life frozen in *ice*.

Coming across these little purply bugs isn't everything Antarctic exploration is hyped up to be, to say the least—researchers have to dig through seal and penguin poop (where nitrogen fertilizer accumulates) to collect their specimens. Unsurprisingly, Antarctic Midges are reported to be pretty stinky *bug*gers.

Masters of Adaptation

Even though they live in what—from a human's POV—might be one of the harshest of Earth's many beautiful and complex environments, the Antarctic Midge is perfectly adapted to its polar home. Midge larvae can survive at temperatures as low as -4.0°F (-20.0°C) and they can survive in both freshwater and saltwater. They can even withstand the loss of up to 70 percent of their body fluids! Researchers say this resilience comes in part from a physiological adaptation called rapid cold hardening, which helps animals survive in freezing temperatures.

(Potential) Medical Marvels

While research is still in its early stages, scientists believe that studying the Antarctic Midge's adaptations for freezing and dehydrating could actually lead to some major human health advancements—specifically, preserving tissue for organ transplants!

underfrog ● fact ●

On average, the Antarctic Midge spends about eight months out of the year frozen in ice and has an adult life span of only a week.

Antarctic Midge, Palmer Station, Antarctica.
Photo © Richard E. Lee Jr.

SEA SLUG

Animal: Sea Slug
Class: Gastropoda (Gastropod)
Species: *Doris kerguelenensis*
Status: Not Assessed
Population Trend: Unknown

These Sea Slugs are large Antarctic nudibranchs, which is a fancy word for shell-less mollusks. The group's scientific order name, *Nudibranchia*, means "naked gills" and describes the feathery gills that most of them have on their backs. Besides looking cool, these "naked gills" are also how Sea Slugs breathe!

Sea Slugs have a wide range—they live all across the Drake Passage, the body of water separating Antarctica from South America, and can be found anywhere from 3–5,000 feet (1–1,550 meters) deep! Sea Slugs are master adapters. They've evolved with their habitat to live in low and relatively stable temperatures, and have even adapted to safely eat sponges that contain toxic chemicals. The Sea Slugs can also create their own toxic chemicals, unlike other nudibranchs, which absorb chemicals from sponges into their own bodies and then taste just as bad to their predators! Pretty ingenious, we'd say.

Nudibranchs are hermaphrodites, meaning they have both female and male sex organs and can fertilize any other individual of the same species. They have a wildly long embryonic period— thirty-six months!—and are what's known as "direct developers," meaning their babies come out fully formed instead of in a larval stage. Experts believe their long embryonic period might be because of their slow metabolism in the cold.

Creating Their Own Chemistry

As far as threats go, very little is known about Sea Slugs. They're subject to climate change, but how it will affect the animal is unknown. Going forward, experts say the next steps are figuring out exactly how many species there are, and then seeing just how closely related they are. While it's definitely far down the road, some people believe that Sea Slugs could potentially cure diseases like leukemia based on their ability to create their own chemistry. Talk about superpowers!

underfrog ●
fact ●

While *Doris kerguelenensis* was thought to be one species for a long time, researchers have discovered that there are actually at least thirty to fifty different species, which were all mistaken for each other!

Sea Slug, water temperature 36.0°F (2.2°C).
Depth, approximately 50 feet (15.25 meters).
Goudier Island, Antarctica. Photo © Kevin Lee

WATER BEAR

Animal: Water Bear
Class: Heterotardigrada (Tardigrade)
Species: *Mopsechiniscus franciscae*
Status: Not Assessed
Population Trend: Unknown

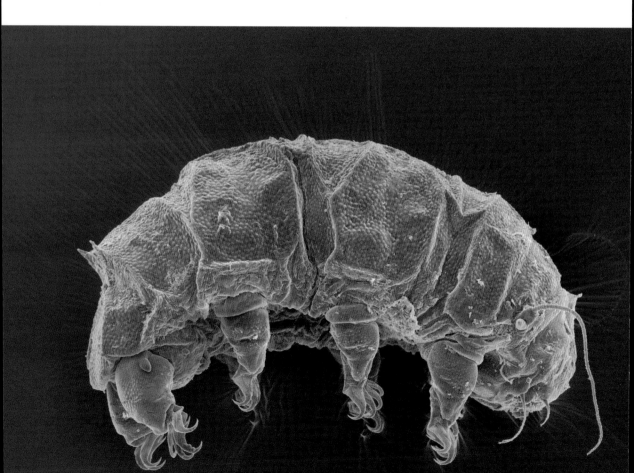

Hailed as "the most indestructible animal on Earth," the microscopic Water Bear—aka the Tardigrade—can basically survive anything when it is dried out (a state called "tun"—just wait, we'll get there!). And we mean ANYTHING—it can go up to thirty years without food or water, survive in both below-freezing *and* boiling temperatures, and has even survived in *outer space*! Plus, it's quite cute and chonky.

Its resiliency has earned the Water Bear the coveted title of *extremophile*, which is an elite group of animals that—to put it simply—can survive things most others can't. Water Bears live in just about every environment and prefer making their terrestrial home in a film of water on mosses and lichens, earning them another less intimidating nickname: "moss piglet."

In 2014, a new "moss piglet" species was discovered in Antarctica: *Mopsechiniscus franciscae*. Like all other Tardigrade species, this one has eight legs. Its only different physical attributes are the reddish pads on its legs and a distinct pattern of hairs on its body. A DNA analysis later confirmed this is a new species.

Survival of the Most Adaptable

Unfortunately, not even the "indestructible" Water Bear is truly indestructible—long-term exposure to oxygen and high temperatures will do them in. They have adapted to make the most of hot, dry conditions by using a survival technique known as cryptobiosis. Cryptobiosis is a state of inactivity the Water Bear snaps into when its habitat is especially dry—it's able to drain all of the water out of its half-millimeter-long body, retract its head and limbs, and roll up into a ball—a dry husk, or "tun" state. When the conditions are more to its liking, the Water Bear unrolls itself and goes about its day! Perhaps this is the reason this animal has been able to survive mass extinctions, ice ages, and everything else that's happened in the last six hundred million years!

underfrog ● fact ●

Tardigrades have been living on Earth for over six hundred million years now (that's four hundred million years before dinosaurs).

Water Bear, color-enhanced scanning electron microscope image.
Photo © Roberto Guidetti, University of Modena and Reggio Emilia, Italy

LEOPARD SEAL

Animal: Leopard Seal
Class: Mammalia (Mammal)
Species: *Hydrurga leptonyx*
Status: Least Concern
Population Trend: Unknown

Named for its black-spotted coat, the Leopard Seal is vastly different from its land-dwelling feline counterpart, but they share many characteristics. It's a fierce predator, and the only seal species that regularly hunts warm-blooded prey (including other seals). It's also the second-largest seal in the Antarctic, after the Southern Elephant Seal, so basically...if you're a penguin and you see one of these guys eyeing you, you're probably in trouble.

The majority of the Leopard Seal's day revolves around hunting. Fish, krill, penguins...you name it. They're known for their sneak attacks, where they hide underwater behind blocks of ice or deep below the surface and then snatch penguins as they dive into the water or rest on the water.

While the Leopard Seal's only natural predator is the Killer Whale, climate change and extractive industries in the Antarctic seem to be its biggest threats.

In 2016, twenty-four countries and the European Union signed an agreement to create the Ross Sea Marine Protected Area (MPA), which will safeguard the Ross Sea from commercial fishing for thirty-five years. Our friends at SeaLegacy are working with the Antarctic and Southern Ocean Coalition (ASOC) and others to promote the creation of more MPAs in Antarctica to help protect the ice and animals like the powerful Leopard Seal from extractive industries.

Droning On

While the Leopard Seal isn't currently listed as Endangered, researchers are staying alert by monitoring their populations with drone cameras. These drones mostly follow them around the western Antarctic Peninsula where the Leopard Seal population is the densest and the ice is melting the fastest.

underfrog ●
fact ●

The Leopard Seal can grow to be up to 12 feet (3.66 meters) long and weigh more than 1,000 pounds (454 kilograms).

Leopard Seal, Lemaire Channel, Antarctica.
Photo © Russ Mittermeier, Re:wild

AUCKLAND RAIL

Animal: Auckland Rail
Class: Aves (Bird)
Species: *Lewinia muelleri*
Status: Vulnerable
Population Trend: Stable

Small. Secretive. Subantarctic. All these words can be used to describe the cheeky little Auckland Rail, a bird known to live on only two of the subantarctic Auckland Islands. Today, their population is estimated to be around two thousand. This little birdie was first documented scientifically in the second half of the nineteenth century, but then it seemingly disappeared. It was considered a lost species for many years up until 1966 when it was rediscovered on Adams Island. In 1993, it was also found on (the unfortunately named) Disappointment Island. But rest assured, this rediscovery is good news!

Life on Disappointment (and Adams) Island

Most experts believe that Auckland Rails once lived on every island in the Auckland Islands group, but vegetation changes from pigs and cattle as well as predation by cats has run them off a couple of the islands, including the main Auckland Island. These days, the rail only lives on Disappointment Island and Adams Island, with about 75 percent of them calling Adams home. With such a small population limited to just two sites, any disturbance to either site could be bad news for the species.

Predator-Free Possibilities

In 2018, New Zealand's Conservation Minister, Eugenie Sage, announced funding for a major pest eradication project on the main Auckland Island. They pledged $2 million over the next three years to fund planning and field trials in hopes of making Auckland Island 100 percent predator-free by 2050!

Even today, Auckland Island is the largest and most biologically diverse archipelago of New Zealand's subantarctic islands. Getting rid of invasive pigs, mice, and cats would let the Auckland Rails, as well as a whole bunch of other native birds—including mighty seabirds like the Antipodean Albatross—breed and nest freely.

Auckland Rail, Antarctica. Photo © Colin O'Donnell

underfrog
fact

The Auckland Rail usually hides in dense tussock grasses and herby
ground vegetation and actually rarely flies!

Antarctic Krill, Antarctica.
Photo © Flip Nicklin, Minden Pictures

ANTARCTIC KRILL

Animal: Antarctic Krill
Class: Malacostraca (Crustacean)
Species: *Euphausia superba*
Status: Least Concern
Population Trend: Stable

While it may only be about 2 inches (5 centimeters) in length, the Antarctic Krill plays a much bigger role in its ecosystem than its little krill brain is able to comprehend. This tiny crustacean is a main food staple for whales, seals, ice fish, penguins, and hundreds of other Antarctic species.

The Antarctic Krill is one of the largest of all eighty-five krill species. Krill can live for up to seven years, which is shocking, considering their position at the top of so many animals' food lists. But then again, they're not exactly low on supply—it's estimated that the Antarctic Krill population ranges from 125 million tons to 6 billion tons in the waters surrounding Antarctica.

Ice Cover Lovers

In a sad turn of events, recent studies have shown that Antarctic Krill numbers could drop by about 80 percent by the end of the century. Scientists say this drop would be the result of major ice cover loss caused by overfishing and climate change. All this ice loss gets rid of one of the Antarctic Krill's favorite meals: ice algae.

Carbon Keepers

In an exciting new discovery, scientists learned that krill are actually capable of removing carbon from the atmosphere. Basically, the Antarctic Krill eats phytoplankton and excretes carbon-rich pellets that sink deep into the ocean, storing it there and contributing nutrients to the ocean floor. All over the entire ocean, swarms of krill transfer about 0.3 million tons of carbon every day. (This is equal to the daily amount of CO_2 emissions of the UK!) Thanks to its carbon-storing abilities, the krill plays a fundamental role in controlling atmospheric carbon levels and does its part to keep the global climate in check.

underfrog ● fact ●

At certain times of the year, Antarctic Krill clump together in such dense, giant swarms that they can be seen from space!

SOUTHERN ELEPHANT SEAL

Animal: Southern Elephant Seal, aka Sea Elephant
Class: Mammalia (Mammal)
Species: *Mirounga leonina*
Status: Least Concern
Population Trend: Stable

Despite being the largest non-cetacean (cetaceans include whales, dolphins, and porpoises) marine mammal in the world, the Southern Elephant Seal doesn't actually get its name from its size—instead, the name comes from the males' distinctive trunk-like nose! Called a "proboscis," this elephant-esque snout helps adult male Southern Elephant Seals produce some ice-shattering roars. These roars come in especially handy when mating season rolls around and the males have to out-alpha all the other males. While some of these "mating battles" only go as far as roaring and puffing their chests out at each other, some can turn into violent and gory authority struggles.

A bull Southern Elephant Seal can be twice as heavy as an adult male Walrus and can be six to seven times the weight of a Polar Bear or Kodiak Bear. Oh yeah, and their trunks can be up to 1.5 feet (0.46 meters) long!

Sometimes called Sea Elephants, these animals give birth in the late winter, with the females popping out one pup each. Over the course of the next three to four weeks, the new mamas don't eat anything or hunt for meals for their babies—instead, they and their little ones survive off of energy stored in the mother's blubber.

Back from the Brink

Southern Elephant Seals produce a lot of blubber to protect their internal organs from the cold. In the past, these mostly subantarctic behemoths were hunted almost to the brink of extinction for that blubber, which could be rendered into oil and then sold. Luckily, because of new legal protections that established their habitat as a marine protected area, they've managed to bounce back. Of course, there are still some things that pose threats for the future—mostly expanding fisheries and, as always, climate change.

underfrog ●
fact ●

Southern Elephant Seals can dive deeper than 5,500 feet
(1,676 meters) and stay underwater for over two hours.

Southern Elephant Seal, Gold Harbour, South Georgia, South Atlantic. Photo © Nick Garbutt/www.nickgarbutt.com

ANTARCTIC DRAGONFISH

Animal: Antarctic Dragonfish, aka Naked Dragonfish

Class: Actinopterygii (Fish)

Species: *Gymnodraco acuticeps*

Status: Not Assessed

Population Trend: Unknown

When you break it down, the Antarctic Dragon-fish's scientific name—*Gymnodraco acuticeps*—gives you a pretty accurate visual description of this animal: *Gymno* = naked; *Draco* = dragon; *Acute* = sharp/pointy; and *Ceps* = head. Also called the Naked Dragonfish, this species is named for its lack of scales. Instead, it has skin! Baring it all in the freezing cold is no easy feat, but these Antarctic nudists have what's called antifreeze glycoproteins in their blood. Thanks to this handy adaptation, the Antarctic Dragonfish can survive in waters as cold as 28.4°F (-2.0°C). In fact, the water it lives in is about 28.5°F (-1.9°C) for the majority of the year.

This species is a carnivorous sit-and-wait predator, using the sharp, backward-pointing canine-like teeth that protrude from its lower jaw to snag small and juvenile fishes in the water. The Antarctic Dragonfish produces a sort of slime when it feels threatened, which may make it slippery—and more difficult—for predators to catch.

Worms, Weddells, and Other Woes

Antarctic Dragonfish often get tangled up in collection nets, and, predators-wise, this species is preyed on by the Giant Antarctic Toothfish and seals (mostly Weddell Seals). Their eggs are also susceptible to being gobbled up when they're left unguarded, most notably by a worm species called the Giant Nemertean. And, of course, climate change also poses a threat since this animal spends a lot of time hanging out in subfreezing water and is adapted to tolerate only minor temperature changes.

All Is Well (for Now)

As far as conservation goes, no real measures have been taken to protect the Antarctic Dragonfish. This fish is not commercially hunted, and any real future threats will most likely be environmentally related. For the moment, at least, all is well for this nudist species.

underfrog ●
fact ●

The Antarctic Dragonfish is the only member of its genus, *Gymnodraco*.

Antarctic Dragonfish, Antarctica.
Photo © Paulo Oliveira, Alamy Stock Photo

ANTARCTIC SILVERFISH

Animal: Antarctic Silverfish
Class: Actinopterygii (Fish)
Species: *Pleuragramma antarctica*
Status: Least Concern
Population Trend: Stable

The Antarctic Silverfish is exactly what you think it would be: a small silver fish that's native to Antarctica. This glimmery herring-like fish can be found just about anywhere in the coastal waters, in spots with pack ice. They can even survive as deep as 3,300 feet (1,000 meters)!

This 5.9-inch (15-centimeter) fish has done what most other species here have to do—it's adapted to Antarctica's frigid and seasonal conditions. It's also managed to become the most dominant fish species where it lives. The Antarctic Silverfish plays an extremely important role in the Antarctic food web, as it really rounds out most large predators' diets. Without this little guy, Antarctic ecosystems would definitely be disrupted.

Sea Ice, Ice Baby

At the moment, the Antarctic Silverfish isn't highly threatened, but, as with any species, climate change does not help its long-term survival. As both adults and larvae, Antarctic Silverfish heavily rely on sea ice for reproduction. As climate change is rapidly melting the ice, the species will come under increasing threat.

Luckily Least Concern

Since it's listed as Least Concern, there are no direct conservation measures in place for this species. But in 2013, the Antarctic Silverfish reproduction area along the Ross Sea coastline, called Silverfish Bay, became an ASPA (Antarctic Specially Protected Area) and is presently part of the Ross Sea Marine Protected Area.

underfrog ● fact ●

The Antarctic Silverfish eats krill and copepods but isn't above resorting to cannibalism when it has to.

Antarctic Silverfish, Antarctica.
Photo © Alfred Wegener Institute

CAMPBELL ISLAND TEAL

Animal: Campbell Island Teal
Class: Aves (Bird)
Species: *Anas nesiotis*
Status: Vulnerable
Population Trend: Stable

The Campbell Island Teal is one of the world's rarest ducks—so rare that it was thought to be Extinct for over one hundred years. This bird is small, flightless, and nocturnal, and is only found on Campbell Island, a completely uninhabited subantarctic island of New Zealand. Its odd evolutionary adaptations are the result of living on a predator-free island that has been isolated from the rest of the world for over eighty million years. The Campbell Island Teal leads a pretty low-key, off-the-grid life!

New Species Not Welcome

These days, the Campbell Island Teal's only real threat is the possibility of introducing predators—*ahem*, cats and rats. (Norwegian Rats brought to the island on sailing ships are what initially drove the teal's numbers so low.) Any new species or even avian diseases showing up could wipe out this entire species easily. However, conservation efforts have been very helpful to this species!

A Pest-Free Paradise

In 1984, after seeing that the Campbell Island Teal population was about to disappear forever, New Zealand's Department of Conservation (DOC) swooped in and took in eleven individuals to start a conservation breeding program. The program found some success in 1994, when Daisy—the first wild female to lay eggs in human care—accepted a mate!

Since then, many captive-bred birds have been released onto Codfish Island, an island about 400 miles (644 kilometers) away, that's intensely managed and 100 percent pest-free. DOC then launched the world's largest rat eradication program on Campbell Island, hoping to become just as pest-free and inviting to its namesake duck as Codfish Island, and HUZZAH! It was a success! Campbell Island was officially declared rat-free in 2003, and birds were successfully reintroduced to the island from the temporary Codfish Island population. Today, the Campbell Island Teal population has reestablished itself and is living comfortably on Campbell Island.

underfrog fact

Even though it can't fly, the Campbell Island Teal can be surprisingly fast on its feet when it feels threatened.

Campbell Island Teal, Campbell Island, New Zealand.
Photo © Ole J. Liodden

COMB JELLY

Animal: Comb Jelly
Class: Tentaculata (Comb Jelly)
Species: *Mertensiid ctenophore*
Status: Not Assessed
Population Trend: Unknown

Are they little deep-sea spaceships? Iridescent rainbow alien-squid hybrids? Or maybe they're what you'd get if a jellyfish fell into a vat of acid and emerged with superpowers? Any way you put it, the Comb Jelly is easily one of the most otherworldly animals on planet Earth.

Comb Jellies get their name from their combs, aka the plates of giant fused cilia that run up and down their bodies. These combs help propel the jelly through the Antarctic waters, acting like tiny oars. These comb rows can even give off a rainbow appearance. Don't confuse this with bioluminescence, though: This rainbow effect occurs when light gets scattered in different directions by the moving cilia!

Although they have the trademark mushroom head and long tentacles, and look a lot like your standard jellyfish, the Comb Jelly actually isn't all that closely related to its fellow gelatinous sea-dwellers. They belong to different phyla (jellyfish to Cnidaria, and Comb Jellies to Ctenophora) and lead completely separate lives.

Sea-Dwelling Climate Regulators

Cnidaria and Ctenophora actually play their own, similar roles in the ocean habitat in which they live. Cnidaria and Ctenophora are climate regulators that help sequester carbon—when they die, their carcasses sink to the ocean floor and transfer carbon from surface waters to the seabed. They themselves are food for other animals. Some experts say they also indirectly contribute to nutrient cycling, which helps ensure there is plenty of plankton for other animals to eat.

Intergalactic and Indestructible

At this time, losing the intergalactic Comb Jelly doesn't seem like much of a possibility. Having been around for more than five hundred million years, this species is pretty much equipped to deal with anything—to a point.

Comb Jelly, McMurdo Sound, Ross Sea, Antarctica. Photo © John B. Weller

underfrog
fact

Unlike jellyfish, Comb Jellies can't sting.

SEA SPIDER

Animal: Sea Spider

Class: Pycnogonida (Arthropod)

Species: *Colossendeis*

Status: Not Assessed

Population Trend: Unknown

Thanks to a phenomenon called polar gigantism, Antarctic sea spiders are huge—and are the newest contenders for your nightmare fuel. With their long, twig-like legs, these marine arthropods can grow to be as big as dinner plates—some even have leg spans of up to 2 feet (61 centimeters)! They are carnivorous and feed by sticking their proboscis into animals and sucking out the juices. Scary, sure, but mostly fascinating.

Sea spiders have some pretty unconventional adaptations too. While they don't have any lungs or gills, sea spiders are able to breathe through their cuticle—their shell-like skin! Since their bodies are pretty small, their intestines actually run through their legs. A recent study has found that sea spiders pump blood by contracting their leg guts, making them the only animal in the world with this bizarre circulatory system.

Hot Water and "Hitchhikers"

Some researchers worry that climate change could really put a damper on giant sea spiders, as they wouldn't fare well in warmer and more acidic waters. However, more recent studies suggest that these spiders' Swiss-cheese-esque skin may be able to sustain them through at least a little bit of warming.

Another potential threat to sea spiders are so-called hitchhikers: things like Stalked Barnacles that hook onto them and obstruct their breathing. These "hitchhikers" also make it harder for sea spiders to move around, and by increasing the spider's surface area, the barnacles make them more prone to being swept away by ocean currents.

Five Hundred Million Years Strong

Sea spiders have had a lot of practice evolving and diversifying over the last five hundred million years, and they even survived the end-Permian mass extinction that wiped out many other marine animals. Only time will tell how these crazy-cool creepy-crawlers do when faced with modern pollutants like microplastics, oil spills, and habitat destruction.

**underfrog ●
fact ●**

There are more than one thousand living species of sea spiders.

Sea Spider, Ross Sea, Antarctica.
Photo © John B. Weller

SOON-TO-BE-POSSIBLY-LOST SPECIES:
ANTARCTIC MINKE WHALE

Animal: Antarctic Minke Whale
Class: Mammalia (Mammal)
Species: *Balaenoptera bonaerensis*
Status: Near Threatened
Population Trend: Unknown

One of the only Baleen Whales (whales that have bristles in their mouths instead of teeth) that lives in the ice-covered Southern Ocean, the Antarctic Minke Whale has masterfully adapted to the harsh Antarctic conditions. This species is all about that sea ice life—it helps itself to the krill that chill under the ice cover, and lingers as close to the ice as possible, where it is more difficult for Orca, one of its predators, to get to it.

Climate change is a big problem for the Antarctic Minke Whales. As temperatures get warmer and the ice in Antarctica melts, feeding will become significantly harder for this big blubbery species. Groups of minkes are often found feeding in and around pack ice, and recent studies have shown that where there is less ice, there are fewer minke whales.

underfrog ●
fact ●

Antarctic Minke Whales are known for their curiosity and for regularly swimming up and "saying hi" to passing ships.

ANTIPODEAN ALBATROSS

Animal: Antipodean Albatross
Class: Aves (Bird)
Species: *Diomedea antipodensis*
Status: Endangered
Population Trend: Decreasing

Move over, Big Bird. The Antipodean Albatross and its two subspecies may not be as tall as the famous yellow bird, but for seabirds they are huge with a wingspan nearly 10 feet (3 meters) in length. Antipodean Albatrosses live only on the smaller islands of New Zealand, including the subantarctic Antipodes Islands. At last count, there were about fifty thousand adult birds, but experts fear the population has dropped rapidly since 2004, earning the species an Endangered classification.

A Deadly Food Fight

One of the main drivers of the Antipodean Albatross population decline seems to be long-line fisheries, especially those seeking Southern Bluefin Tuna. The birds follow the boats and take bait from the hooks, which results in the same unwitting fate as the fish the lines are meant to catch. Female birds are more likely to suffer this fate, which has also led to an imbalance of males and females in the Antipodean Albatross population—making it harder for male birds to find a date and ensure a new generation of albatrosses. If fishing continues at this rate, this bird could find itself on a most wanted lost species list in coming years.

But conservationists are on the case! Since 1969, thousands of chicks have been banded on Antipodes and Adams Islands so that experts can track survival rates and population trends. They are also working to reduce fisheries' bycatch by making sure the fisheries are following regulations meant to help keep the birds and other bycatch species safe, and monitoring new fisheries.

underfrog ● fact ●

Courting pairs perform elaborate
dances and wild calls to impress their
potential new beau or belle.

IAN HOGG

Name: Dr. Ian Hogg
Antarctic Springtail Expert
Title: Ecologist
Organization: Polar Knowledge Canada

When it comes to microscopic Antarctic animals, there is one name in particular that may come to mind: Dr. Ian Hogg. Dr. Hogg is an ecologist with Polar Knowledge Canada, a federal research organization that advances Canadian leadership in the ever-fascinating world of polar science and technology. Ian's personal area of expertise is the Antarctic Springtail.

The Antarctic Springtail is a primitive, wingless insect relative called an arthropod. It has six legs and gets around on the rocky landscape by crawling or floating on meltwater. While

Dr. Ian Hogg, Korea Polar Research Institute (KOPRI) field camp, Cape Hallett in northern Victoria Land, East Antarctica. Photo © Wanho Lim

they're smaller than sesame seeds, these species have somehow survived thirty ice ages! In 2018, Dr. Hogg was one of the people who rediscovered *Tullbergia mediantarctica*, a species of Antarctic Springtail that hadn't been seen since 1964. For Dr. Hogg and his colleagues, rediscovering this springtail and studying it is all about witnessing an animal and its ecosystem changing along with the climate. And what subject could be better than a thirty-time ice age survivor?

MICHELLE LARUE

Name: Dr. Michelle LaRue
Penguin Expert
Title: Ecologist
Organization: University of Canterbury in New Zealand

If you're looking for some high-resolution satellite images of Antarctic animals, look no further than Dr. Michelle LaRue. Dr. LaRue has photographed Emperor Penguins, Adélie Penguins, Weddell Seals, Polar Bears, Muskoxen—you name it, she's taken a satellite image of it! Today, she's spearheading a new method of monitoring population dynamics out of New Zealand's University of Canterbury that is great for observing how different species of animals react when their environment changes.

Dr. LaRue has been a part of a bunch of "species from space" studies (not aliens, but satellites!), including one that uncovered Emperor Penguin colonies from their giant poop stains seen in one of the satellite images. Dr. LaRue's work with these "species from space" images is an

Dr. Michelle LaRue, Cape Crozier, Antarctica. Photograph obtained within the requisite Antarctic Conservation Act permits and from a safe distance to avoid disturbing wildlife. Photo © Brad Herried

awesome, noninvasive way for us to learn which penguin colonies are thriving and which are close to collapse. Without Dr. LaRue, we'd be completely in the dark when it comes to many Antarctic animals—and their miles and miles of poop.

Index

Note: Page numbers in **bold** indicate summary lists of animals by continent.

About the Author

Re:wild is on a mission to protect and restore the wild. We have a singular and powerful focus: the wild as the most effective solution to the interconnected climate, biodiversity, and pandemic crises. Re:wild is a force multiplier that brings together Indigenous peoples, local communities, influential leaders, nongovernmental organizations, governments, corporations, and the public to protect and rewild at the scale and speed we need. Re:wild launched in 2021 based on more than three decades of combined conservation impact of the Leonardo DiCaprio Foundation and Global Wildlife Conservation, leveraging expertise, partnerships, and platforms under one unified brand, bringing new attention, energy, and voices together. Our vital work has protected and conserved over twelve million acres, benefitting more than sixteen thousand species in the world's most irreplaceable places for biodiversity. We don't need to reinvent the planet. We just need to rewild it—for all wildkind. Learn more at rewild.org.

About the Freelancer

Growing up in a house full of dogs, cats, and one Beta fish that lived for more than five years, Syd Robinson has always had a deep love for animals. So much so that she eventually became one of *BuzzFeed*'s top animal writers, constantly living in the wild world of Internet pets! When she's not working on a new *BuzzFeed* post, Syd draws, buys too many plants, and writes music under the name Ghostcamp. She currently lives in Manhattan with her naughty pug, Phoebe.